As I Saw It
A Sighted Daughter's Memoir of Growing Up With Blind Parents

by Laura Schriner

Copyright © 2016 Laura Schriner

All rights reserved. No part of this book may be reproduced in any form without permission in writing from the author. Reviewers may quote brief passages in reviews.

ISBN: 978-0-692-69030-7

DISCLAIMER

No part of this publication may be reproduced or transmitted in any form or by any means, mechanical or electronic, including photocopying or recording, or by any information storage and retrieval system, or transmitted by email without permission in writing from the author.

Neither the author nor the publisher assumes any responsibility for errors, omissions, or contrary interpretations of the subject matter herein. Any perceived slight of any individual or organization is purely unintentional.

Cover Design: John Matthews and Carolyn Sheltraw

Editing: Kate Makled & Maggie McReynolds

*To my mom and dad; because without them, there wouldn't be a book. In loving memory of my dad......
88s, Dad, I miss you!*

Table of Contents

Chapter 1: Serendipity—The Story of Roy and Diane 1

Chapter 2: Up to the Accident—Before I Knew Him as Dad 15

Chapter 3: Little Miss Independent—Before I Knew Her as Mom 33

Chapter 4: Life at Blind School 51

Chapter 5: Just Starting Out—Making New Lives Together 63

Chapter 6: Subtle Differences of Operation 79

Chapter 7: Being Me, Seeing Things Differently 95

Chapter 8: School Days, Kids and Dad Alike 107

Chapter 9: The Things I Got Away With. . . or Not 119

Chapter 10: Things That Only Happen in a Blind Family ...133

Chapter 11: The Judgment of It All 149

Chapter 12: Fulfilled Lives, Keeping Busy 161

Chapter 13: Where We Are Now 175

Conclusion 183

Acknowledgements 187

About the Author 189

Chapter 1
Serendipity — The Story of Roy and Diane

ROY WAS ONLY 26 YEARS OLD WHEN he first arrived at the Orientation Center for the Blind (OCB) in Oakland, California. He entered the blind school so he could learn how to take care of himself and learn skills to live and adjust to his new life of blindness. He was involved in a tragic accident just months prior that left him with no vision at all. It was one of those accidents that happened so quickly nothing could have been done to stop it. Worse, it had happened when he was all alone in the garage. So it seemed like an eternity before anyone heard his screams for help. By the time help arrived, the damage had been done, and his vision was gone. The doctors told him there wasn't any surgery or other treatment that could be done to bring back the slightest bit of sight. His world was total darkness, and he needed to learn how to deal with it.

That's why his doctors pretty much forced him into the blind school so soon after the accident, even though his wounds weren't totally healed. That's what doctors did back in 1959. Instead of getting psychological help to deal with the accident, injuries, and sudden blindness, his doctors thought he needed to keep his mind busy so that he didn't have time to ruminate about the accident and dwell on thoughts of being blind. The doctors believed he needed to keep his mind on constructive things, and wanted him to be around other blind people, instead of spending time alone letting negative thoughts creep into his head. So off to OCB he went.

When he arrived at OCB, he lived in a standard dorm-type room like all the rest of the students. The rooms were similar to any college-type dorm room except each student at OCB had his or her own room, which was about the size of a bedroom and contained a bed that was wedged into one of the corners of the room with a nightstand alongside the bed. The room also had a small closet, a little larger than a typical hallway coat closet, where he could hang his clothes. There was also a built-in chest of drawers where he could put his undergarments, t-shirts, socks, and anything else he wanted to tuck away. The room was completed with a small, table-like desk and a chair. There was no running water in the rooms, so he had to use the community showers and bathroom that were just a few short steps away.

On the second day in his new surroundings, he was awakened by a tickling sensation across his face. Only half awake, he brushed his face with his hands and noticed that his hands started to get the same tickling sensation. It wasn't long before he realized that the tickling sensation he was feeling were ants crawling across his body. The ants had been attracted to the still-weeping wounds from the accident that left him blind and had crawled on him while he slept. Feeling helpless, he called out for help and rushed outside his room in his underwear. Someone immediately grabbed his arm, and for that split second, he was relieved not to be alone.

The stranger rushed him into the shower to rinse the ants from his body. Someone from the school came to the room to exterminate the ants. Someone else brought him fresh clothes to change into, while he sat outside until he was sure all the ants were gone from his room so he wouldn't have to worry about them again.

A few months later, he had learned to get around a little bit on his own with the use of his cane. Restless one night, because the night-owl lifestyle he had as a sighted man had not really changed after going blind, he ventured out by himself to get something to eat to help him fall asleep. He grabbed his red-tipped cane, locked his dorm room, and ventured out into the cool night air. He headed to the only place he knew was open at 2:00 a.m., the all-night diner that he had been to many times before. It was only a couple blocks away. "I'll grab a burger and come right back so I can make it to classes tomorrow," he thought. Unfortunately, his evening didn't go as planned, and he never made it to the diner. You see, Roy didn't have the best of luck back then, and we've all heard that bad luck and tragedy always strikes in threes. Going blind was tragedy number one, and tragedy number two was literally just around the corner.

Roy was across the street from the diner, and the smell of char-broiled hamburgers lingered in the air as he waited on the corner for the traffic light to turn green so that he could cross the street. The traffic light turned green, and he took a few steps into the street. The car came out of nowhere fast, and there was no time to react. Roy was down in an instant. Thank goodness there was a witness who saw the whole thing. The single witness to the hit-and-run accident ran over to Roy to see if he was okay, but Roy was just lying there, unconscious and lifeless in the middle of the road.

The driver didn't see him, nor did the driver stop after he was hit. If it wasn't for this witness, Roy could have been left there to die.

The witness said he had been watching Roy walk down the street for a couple of minutes. He watched Roy step up to the intersection, press the button on the streetlight to go across the street, and wait for the light to turn green. It wasn't hard for Roy to know when the traffic light turned green, because all the traffic lights near the blind school buzzed audibly to let the blind students know the light was green and that it was safe to cross. I know that he paused and listened to make sure that the cross-traffic had actually stopped, too, because that is an important part of learning how to cross the street when you are blind. And now Roy, who had just gone blind a few months earlier, had more problems than just the loss of his sight to worry about.

An ambulance came and took Roy to the County Hospital in Oakland, CA. It's the place where people who don't have insurance, or very little resources to be able to afford medical care, are usually taken for treatment. And that was a pretty appropriate choice for Roy at this time in his life because he hadn't been able to work since going blind. He didn't have any money saved up. Heck, he was just starting to get his life together and only working part-time while he attended community college *before* the accident. Paying for school was just about all he could afford with his part-time job while he was still living at home.

Roy was rushed into surgery immediately upon his arrival at the hospital, so that doctors could repair his shattered leg. The bumper and grille of the car that hit Roy had rammed into his thigh and had broken the strongest bone in his body, his femur. The car that hit him was typical for a car made in the 1950s, one of those very powerful and heavy muscle cars, solidly made of metal bodies and metal bumpers, unlike the fiberglass cars of today. So Roy was pretty fortunate that he wasn't hurt more severely, and the doctors were able to save his leg.

Roy didn't remember anything about the accident. He awoke all alone in a quiet room where he could only hear people talking in the distance. His body ached, and he didn't know exactly what was wrong. He tried to sit up and touch where the pain was, so he could figure out what was going on, but he could hardly move. So he reached his hand towards the pain, but all he felt there was a hard white plaster cast that circled around his waist and hips. He stretched his hand as far as he could and felt the cast go down his leg. He had started to panic when a nurse suddenly appeared in his room. She told him that he had been hit by a car but that he was safe in a hospital.

Roy asked her what was wrong, and she said, "Mr. Phelps, your leg was broken badly in the car accident. The doctors performed surgery to fix your leg. You have a cast around your body so that your leg can't move, to give the bone in your leg time to set properly and heal." She also said he was going to be in the hospital until his leg could heal enough to get a smaller cast. He needed to be able to get up and walk around on his own before he could leave. Roy knew that he wasn't going to be leaving this hospital room any time soon.

The days were long, made longer because Roy hadn't had enough time to adjust to the darkness of losing his sight in the first place. There wasn't much to do but lie awake in bed most of the day. He hadn't really learned how to do very much on his own yet since going blind, hadn't learned enough Braille to read any books, and he couldn't even see to gawk at the people who walked past his room. He only had a small TV to listen to and keep his mind busy, and the occasional visit from nurses and doctors who wandered into his room.

He rarely had visitors, partly because he didn't know very many people at the blind school, and partly owing to the fact that his family lived far away. His mother worked two jobs to support herself, and she was just barely making it on her own. So it was hard for his mother to take any time off to come see him. His father wasn't around anymore. His older brother had joined the Air Force and was out of the country. His older sister wasn't able to visit, either.

There was no one else in his room, because the hospital didn't want to put anyone sighted next to him since he had so recently gone blind. He was pretty much alone in the quietness of his room for most of the day, at least until his leg healed enough to change to a smaller cast so he could move around on his own. For the most part, the days in the hospital were spent alone in silence with only his thoughts, scattered and uncertain thoughts about this new life of darkness he had yet to figure out, and now a badly broken leg.

• • • • • •

Diane arrived at OCB a few months before Roy. She was finally at the place in her life where she would learn the skills she needed so that she could live on her own and take care of herself. I can only imagine what a stressful but exciting time it was for her. I mean, when she was through with school, she would have her first apartment and live without the help of her parents, siblings, or anyone else. She was going to be making her own rules and be able to do things the way she wanted. Who wouldn't be excited, right? She was already kind of living on her own in the dormitory at other blind schools, but this school was very different from those she had attended when she was younger.

Diane was an adult now, and instead of learning history and math or any of the other academic subjects they taught at the other blind schools, she was here to simply learn life skills, the ones that would allow her to live independently. Going back to live with her family after this was not an option that she wanted; she was determined to make it on her own. From this day forward, her life was going to be different too. She was going to have to learn to accomplish things truly on her own for the first time in her life, and she felt she was up for the challenge.

One of the first people Diane met at the blind school was another student named Josie, who was born blind just like Diane. They were around the same age and hit it off instantly. They were like two peas in a pod. It was just one of those easy relationships that was meant to be. They started off as best friends the moment they met, and their friendship has never ended.

One of the early classes they took together was mobility training. This class was intended to teach them how to get around on their own. It would help both Diane and Josie build the confidence and skills they needed to be totally independent travelers, to go where ever they wanted when they wanted, without having to take someone's arm for help. What they were going to learn in this class was not small stuff by any means. This training would allow them to travel in public by themselves, walk around town to go shopping, navigate restaurants to get something to eat, and travel using the bus and taxi system all by themselves instead of waiting or relying on sighted people. Even some sighted people are afraid to learn these things on their own, so I know that for the blind, the thought of doing it all by themselves was both terrifying and exhilarating at the same time. They were about to embark on a journey to learn some of the most important skills needed for their lives ahead.

Josie and Diane were paired together as mobility partners by their instructor, Pete. They were similarly skilled: both able to get around a little on their own before coming to this school, with a similar overall mobility skill level. Since they were both born blind, they had learned to do some things on their own when they were little, and had adapted quite a bit. They were each able to easily get around the dorms by themselves so that they could visit the other students in the building, and they had no trouble walking to and from the cafeteria on their own. It was the perfect pairing to start their training together.

They had two mobility tasks each day to accomplish together, and Pete was responsible for giving them these tasks. Good ole' Pete, they used to call him. Pete loved all his students, and all the students loved him. He was well-suited for the role: kind and reassuring as he gently taught them how to get around on their own. His sense of humor helped them smooth over some of the toughest and most frustrating times, when they just didn't think they could do it. Diane and Josie were lucky to have such a caring person teaching them how to get around.

The mobility challenges started out small at first, like getting around the school together with their partner to find the different buildings on campus. They had to repeat the same tasks until they were both comfortable with completing them. Once they were comfortable, though, the tasks became just a little bit harder. After learning the campus, they headed off campus to learn more.

The first off-campus task was to walk from campus to a store or restaurant nearby. Then, they graduated to being dropped off a couple of blocks from school, and challenged to find their way back. I don't want you to think that the blind students were just dropped off somewhere, and then someone was waiting for them back at school. The tasks were gradual so that each of the students would feel comfortable before moving on. Students were told at what intersection they were being dropped off, and they knew in which direction the school was located. It was easier than you might think to keep track of the streets around the school, because the layout of the streets formed a grid. The alphabet street names all ran parallel to each other in one direction, and the intersecting streets were all numbers. When the students were dropped off, they would get instructions as to which direction they needed to walk, and they would know how many streets they needed to cross, based on the intersection named.

At first, the students were monitored without their knowledge during the whole trip. As their skill levels improved, the students were monitored less closely. Their tasks were based on their proven abilities, but Pete also sometimes pushed them out of their comfort zones a little more when he thought they could handle it. Pete drove an old beater of a car that sounded like no other. The rattling and rambling noises that Pete's car made could be heard blocks away before his car could actually be seen. The blind students could identify it quite readily. When Pete dropped off Diane and Josie for their mobility tasks away from campus and told them, "See you guys when you get back to campus," they knew he wasn't telling the truth. After all, they could hear his car when he drove by, checking on them. They'd hear his car in the distance and when it got close enough, they'd yell out, "Hello, Pete!" He would yell back, "Doing great, ladies. I'll see you back at school." Pete was usually never very far away when they were first learning how to get around. And that's what made him such a great instructor: all the students felt assured that he had their backs, and he would come to their rescue if they really needed help.

Diane and Josie became proficient in their mobility training, and Pete had started to give them tasks using the public transportation buses. Pete always told them which bus they were to get on, gave them Brailled cards with instructions, told them where they were getting on the bus, and then would tell them the destination, which was usually back at the blind school. He would drive them to the location to catch the bus, and wait to make sure they got on the right bus. Sometimes, he would sneak onto the bus just to watch them and make sure they were okay and doing the right things.

Diane and Josie would get on the bus and tell the bus driver where they needed to get off. They'd always try to sit close to the front so they could hear the driver. The bus drivers announced the name of the next stop just after the bus started in motion from the previous stop. So Diane and Josie would listen to the bus driver call out the stops to know when to get off. Every once in a while, bus drivers didn't call out the stops, so Diane and Josie would have to tell the bus driver where they were going. Usually, the bus drivers were pretty good at keeping track of them, but every once in a while they'd find out the bus driver forgot and they had missed their stop.

Mobility tasks got more and more involved, sometimes having to take multiple buses. They would have to get off of one bus by themselves, and make sure to catch the correct connecting bus. Sometimes it was at the same bus stop, other times they'd have to cross the street or walk a block or two to catch the next bus. The Oakland bus system was great, because if they happened to miss one of the buses, another one would usually come around just a few minutes later. Diane and Josie were getting pretty accustomed to traveling together and had become very proficient using the busses.

One day, they got a task that was like no other they had before. Pete said, "Here you go, ladies—your task for today," as he handed Diane and Josie some bus money and the Brailled index cards with the written details of their task. Pete told Diane and Josie that they were going to visit a guy from school who was in the hospital. He told them:

"One of the students from school has just been involved in a horrible accident and is going to be at the hospital for quite some time. His family lives far away, so he is all alone. His name is Roy Phelps. I want you two to go visit him; be a friend to him and see if he needs anything."

So off they went, just like with any other task they'd had before. Josie and Diane got on the bus, and when the bus driver called out, "County Hospital," they got off the bus. They listened to where all the other people were headed, and followed them inside the hospital. Inside the hospital, they asked for directions to Roy's room. When they got into the elevator, one of the gentleman asked them, "What floor, ladies?" and they rode the elevator up to the floor he was on. They walked out of the elevator and headed down the hallway toward Roy's room.

Roy was lying in bed when he heard a *tap-tap-tap* sound coming from down the hall outside his room. His ears perked up, because that sound was a very familiar sound—he knew it from the blind school. It was the tap of a cane, which could only mean another blind person was here at the hospital. "I wonder if they are coming to see me," he thought to himself, while wondering who it could be, because he didn't know very many people at school yet. Then he heard a laugh. It was the same laugh that he had heard at school—it must be one of the girls at school that he had heard many times in the hallway, but it belonged to a girl that he did not know. He thought to himself expectantly, "It sure sounds like her." Little did he know, that it was the same girl—the girl whose laugh Roy developed a crush on even though he had not even met her.

"Roy," they called out when they got to his room.

"Yes," he said.

"It's Diane and Josie from school. We came to visit."

The nurse in the room showed Diane and Josie to the chairs where they could sit down. They spent hours chatting about school, and all that was going on while he had been out. They told jokes and were having a good time visiting. Roy was having a great time. It wasn't every day that two single girls came to his room to visit him. He was having such a good time he started to forget about his leg.

Josie and Diane stayed for a few hours before they headed back to school on the bus. Roy could hardly believe that the girl who he had heard laughing in the hallways at school, the girl whose laugh he had just about fallen in love with, had just come to visit him in the hospital. Her name was Diane.

Diane and Josie came to visit Roy a few more times over the next three months, which was how long Roy was in the hospital.

It was these early visits in the hospital that sparked a love that was about to blossom!

Chapter 2
Up to the Accident—Before I Knew Him as Dad

ROY WASN'T BORN BLIND, OF COURSE. IN fact, he was born with perfect sight. The accident that caused his blindness didn't happen until he was in his mid-20s. He surely didn't have an easy life growing up by any standards, however. He was born in the South, in Morrilton, Arkansas, in 1933. This part of his story probably isn't much different from most other children growing up in rural families during The Great Depression, but I never really paid too much attention to Roy's early life. I only knew him as Dad.

I was a curious child, and used to ask him questions all the time to get him to talk about his childhood. It wasn't until later, when I really started contemplating my own life, that I realized what a hard childhood he'd really had.

Roy was born one of a set of fraternal twins. He and his twin brother, Coy, had an older brother, Phil, and an older sister, Pauline. They lived in a rural part of Arkansas on a farm, where their mother, (my grandmother) Ellon, did all the farm work while their father (my grandfather), Ethan, searched for work. Both

Ellon and Ethan had only eighth grade educations, which was pretty standard for where they lived and the time they were born, but that also meant that life was that much harder having parents that couldn't find a lot of work and didn't earn very much money. Not having Ethan around very often was also hard on Ellon and the kids. But Ethan was simply trying to take care of his family the best he could, the best he knew how. He took any and all odd jobs, whenever and wherever, just to make whatever money he could to help the family survive.

Figure 1: Roy's Siblings. Top left to right: Pauline and Phil, and bottom left to right, Roy and twin brother, Coy

With Ethan always looking for work, Ellon was left at home to take care of the kids and the farm entirely on her own. Ellon worked exhaustive days and got very little sleep. She had two jobs, in essence. She woke up early to feed the kids and get them off to school, then she would head out to do the work on the farm. She milked the cows, fed the animals, collected eggs from the chickens, weeded and watered the garden, and cooked all the meals for the family. The kids all had to work on the farm and help out with family chores, too. After they all came home from school, the boys would help out on the farm while Roy's sister Pauline helped out inside the house. The boys cleaned up animal pens, brought water to the animals, and made sure everything was all okay on the farm, while Pauline cleaned and helped Ellon with whatever she needed inside.

There was no running water on the farm except for an outside pump. Roy and his siblings took turns pumping water for inside the house and for the animals on the farm. In the summers, when Roy and his twin brother were young, they would take baths outside in large metal tubs because it was so much easier using the water outside than having to carry heavy containers of it inside the house to bathe.

Figure 2: Roy (left) and his twin brother taking baths outside

Even though the kids had to work and times were tough financially, the family still had time for a little fun on their farm. All of the siblings played outside together with the animals, and had lots of room to roam around. Roy's favorite animal to play with was his pig, Salimony. Indeed, Salimony was the first animal that Roy rushed out to check on when he got home from school, and the last one that got his attention before he came in for supper.

Roy's family pretty much lived off the farm as much as they could. They used what little money they earned through Ethan's labor to purchase things they didn't have on the farm. They didn't have much money to buy clothes, or to spend on anything other than necessities. There was only enough money to eat and pay the bills. Roy and his twin brother wore hand-me-down clothing from his older brother, which their mother stitched together when things tore, or patched when it got holes. Patches were common on clothing Roy had to wear back then, because buying new or even gently used clothing put too much of a burden on the family.

Eating, shelter, and health were the main concerns, and anything more wasn't an option for many of the years when Roy was young.

Times got tougher when Ethan couldn't find any work at all. The family had to survive by slaughtering the animals on the farm so that they would have enough to eat. The first to go was Roy's pig, Salimony. Ellon didn't tell the kids what was going to happen, but she needed to put the food on the table. One day after school, Roy rushed out to Salimony's pen as usual to find out that he wasn't around. He ran inside, asking his mom where Salimony was, and she told him that Salimony had to be killed for food so the family could eat. Roy was heartbroken and mad at his mother. He couldn't believe that his pig had been slaughtered. Roy refused to eat his pet pig for the first few nights. Then he became so hungry that he felt forced to eat Salimony, so he wouldn't go hungry another night. Roy was traumatized by the incident, and he cried the whole time he ate. Playing on the farm was never the same for Roy without his pet pig. Those were the toughest times that Roy and his family had to live through.

Ethan had been travelling outside of town, looking for work far and wide, but there didn't seem to be any jobs around the area. Everyone in the area was having the same problem. Ethan heard rumors that jobs were plentiful out west, so he left his family and traveled to California in search of work. He caught a train and rode the rails for days, stopping in different towns along the way to find odd jobs just so he could earn enough to eat and send a little bit of money back home to Ellon and the kids. Ethan finally made it to California, and after a few months he was able to find steady work on the farms in Salinas, a town that consisted of mostly farmland back then. After a few months, he had raised enough money for the rest of the family to finally join him. They all headed out to California in the summer of 1945, when Roy was only nine years old, once all the kids had finished school for the year.

Ethan was able to find plenty of work for a while when they first moved out to California, but the work was seasonal. He even found enough work so that Ellon was able to stay home with the kids for a while. But then work started getting harder and harder to find, and Ethan had to constantly travel to find work again. Ellon's time for staying home ended, and she, too, had to start working outside the home. Roy and his siblings were left alone most of the time because Ellon had to work locally, and Ethan was travelling around taking odd jobs again.

Roy was a good kid when he first moved to California, and he was close to his siblings, especially his twin brother. He got good grades, and his teachers often remarked that he was a bright young boy. He volunteered for the School Safety Patrol before and after school, helping his classmates safely cross the street. After elementary school, though, he had more time on his hands. Unfortunately, he started to hang out with the wrong crowd as a teenager. His relationship with his siblings started to deteriorate, and they all grew farther apart. His older siblings left home. He started getting into fights with the other kids, and started stealing from stores. When his parents found out, it would always mean the belt was coming next, and his relationship with his dad started to become strained.

Roy got along with his mom for the most part, but his dad was gone most of the time. When dad came home, he wasn't a "nice" dad either. He was frustrated and tired. He would punish all the kids for all the bad things they had done while he was gone. So Roy and his siblings started dreading when their dad was supposed to come home. I only heard stories, but the punishment wasn't just a single spanking with the belt. My father and his siblings were horribly beaten, leaving them bruised and sometimes even bloodied. Ethan had a short temper, and he punished them all for any wrong that they did; sometimes there wasn't even a clear incident to prompt the punishment.

The beatings caused Roy's behavior to get even more out of hand, and Roy found himself getting deeper and deeper into trouble. The bond he had with all his siblings, especially his twin brother, deteriorated a great deal, and Roy started hanging out with just his friends. Roy and his friends were known as the "hoodlums" of the town. The police became involved with most of the antics of Roy and his buddies. The police were constantly bringing Roy home in a police car, or calling his parents down to the station to come pick him up. That's what the police did back then. Wayward kids were picked up and let go to their parents for consequences. Teenagers didn't get arrested and charged with crimes as adults; there weren't a lot of juvenile proceedings. The police left it up to the parents to punish their own children, and his dad surely took care of that.

One of the worst crimes Roy committed was stealing a safe from the neighborhood store. Roy and his friends broke into the store, somehow got the safe into a truck, and took it to a garage where they all disassembled it and split the money. No one ever found out about it, so he never got caught or punished. It was a hard time in Roy's life. His hoodlum life lasted for quite a few years, and during that time, he managed to push all of his siblings out of his life. Actually, he had pushed most everyone out of his life that loved and cared for him, except for his mother.

A few of years after graduating high school and shortly after stealing the safe, Roy grew exhausted by constantly getting into trouble and grew tired of his friends and wasting his life. He wanted something more and realized that he was hanging around with people that were going nowhere. At that point, Roy decided he really wanted to do something meaningful in his life. He tried to repair the damaged relationships with his siblings, but they were older and starting their own lives. The relationships with his siblings had deteriorated to the point that they were beyond repair. Roy struggled with the decisions that he had made in his life, but was still determined to make his life better. He searched for work to occupy his time so he could make money instead of steal it.

Figure 3: Roy's high school graduation picture ~1951

Over the next five or six years, Roy worked several odd jobs. He fixed lockers and repaired typewriters at the local high school, and cleaned carpets and rugs in homes. After a while, he grew bored doing odd jobs. He wanted to find something more permanent in his life, so he searched for a full-time job. He was hired by the local hospital as an orderly. He would wheel patients around on gurneys to and from surgeries, and transport people in wheelchairs to x-rays or other tests. Every once in a while, he would also have to transfer a dead person down to the morgue in the basement. A special elevator was used for this, and Roy would take the dead person, covered by a sheet and secured on a gurney, into the elevator. He would then have to ride in the elevator with the dead person down to the basement to hand them off to workers in the morgue. In the daytime, it wasn't so bad, but he was spooked to do it at night.

He used to tell me stories about the hospital job. One time, a dead person "exhaled" a breath when Roy was taking him down the elevator. Roy told me that a lot of the time, a dead person's body would twitch and seemingly move under the sheet. The first time this happened, Roy thought someone was playing a joke on him, and he lifted up the sheet. But it wasn't a joke. Someone had to explain to him that recently deceased people occasionally twitched and moved, and some might even exhale their last breath sometime after death. Roy couldn't get used to that, and so that part of the job was one he definitely didn't like. He was shaken up and creeped out every time he had to take a person down to the morgue. Thank goodness, it was a relatively rare occurrence.

Figure 4: Roy in his hospital orderly uniform

Roy soon grew bored by being an orderly, and wanted something more in his life. He needed a change, and wanted to do something in life that mattered. He wanted to be able to use his brain, and could not embrace the idea of continually working meaningless jobs for the rest of his life. He thought the only way to start was by taking classes at the local community college, so he enrolled and started the next semester. He was excited to be in school during the day, and continued working nights at the hospital.

Life was starting to improve for Roy at that point. He felt like he was actually doing something positive, which was a feeling he hadn't had in a long time, and he enjoyed providing for himself. He was making enough money to pay for school and books, with a little extra to go out and have some fun. He even met a girl in one of his classes, and took her out on several dates. His life was starting to feel good. He still wasn't sure where school would take him, but he knew he was on the right path. He told himself that he'd figure out what he wanted to do after he got a few more classes under his belt. A new semester was right around the corner, with a new set of classes to take. He was discovering himself and his talents for the first time, without a lot of the pressures of his younger years.

His favorite class of the second semester was chemistry; it challenged him the most. It was hard, but he was learning a lot, and he liked that. Other classes seemed to bore him, so he welcomed an opportunity to be challenged and use his brain. Everyone always told him he was smart, because he was always fixing things around the house and tinkering with everything he could get his hands on. He was now starting to feel what everyone had been saying might be true. He was also able to get a better job at a cement factory working with chemists, because he was taking the chemistry class. His job was to clean up the lab, put away chemicals and instruments, and do whatever else the chemists wanted from an assistant. The chemists were easy to work with, and they took him under their wings. They would explain what they were doing and get him involved in their work while he was there. He really liked his job at the cement factory, and the ability to learn from the chemists while helping out, much better than wheeling people around at the hospital—especially the dead ones!

Roy had really started to turn his life around. Just a few years prior, he was getting into trouble, committing petty crimes, and had no direction. Now, he had a plan and everything was coming together. He could finally start planning for the future because he now knew what he wanted in life. He liked working with the chemists at the cement factory so much that he decided to major in chemistry at college. He was feeling so good about his life that he asked the girl that he had been dating for her hand in marriage, and she said yes. It was happy times for the both of them. He was happy that his life was finally settling down after all the trouble he had made for himself in the past.

Life started to become easier for him. Every day wasn't the struggle that he had felt in the past. He was glad to leave behind his hoodlum days, because now life was so much better this way. He had a good job by then, one where he could continue working after he graduated. He was learning things faster in chemistry because of what the chemists were teaching him at the cement factory—so his chemistry classes became a breeze. He was getting the highest grade in the class, and he was excited for his future for the first time in his life.

One day in chemistry class, his instructor was lecturing on the theory and outcome of an experiment. Roy questioned the instructor because he didn't believe what the instructor had said about the experiment was correct. The instructor disagreed, so Roy sat through the rest of class, thinking that something wasn't right with what the instructor had just said. The next day at work, he talked to the chemists, and they agreed with Roy that the instructor must have been mistaken. So Roy thought to himself, "All the chemicals for that experiment, I can get at work. I'm going to prove the chemistry instructor was wrong." So he took the chemicals that he needed for the experiment home from work with him—without the knowledge of the chemists.

Chemistry class was still a couple days away, so he stored the chemicals safely in the garage, out of the way, so no one would find them and get hurt. He grabbed the extension ladder in the garage and leaned it up against the shelf, intending to store the chemicals up high so no one could reach them. He was concerned because one of the chemicals he had taken was sulfuric acid, the type of acid that burns holes through cement. He wanted to be careful putting away the chemicals, so he made two trips up the ladder. He needed one hand to hold onto the ladder while he used his other hand to safely hold the chemicals. He placed the bottles at the back of the shelf so no one could see, even though he was going to use them the very next day. He went off to bed thinking about the experiment and how he was going to prove his instructor wrong.

Roy woke up the next day and had a big, leisurely breakfast. He didn't have to work that day, and his classes weren't until later, so he slept in and waited until his mom left for work before he got up. After breakfast, he went into the garage and grabbed the ladder that was again standing upright against the wall. He leaned the ladder against the shelf where he had put the chemicals, and climbed up the ladder to retrieve them. He made a couple of trips up the ladder to bring down the chemicals one at a time, just like he had done to put them away. He placed the chemicals on the workbench and got out the notes from his chemistry class, because he wanted to make sure he did the experiment just as the instructor explained in class. How else was he going to prove him wrong if he didn't do it exactly as explained?

Roy mixed all the chemicals together in the right amounts. Pretty soon, a big smile started to appear on Roy's face, because his suspicions were right. The reaction was nothing like the instructor said in class—it turned out just like Roy thought. He had just proved his instructor totally wrong, and was on cloud nine. He couldn't wait to go back to class to tell the instructor what he found out from the experiment that he'd replicated in his garage.

He cleaned up the area where was working, and put all the chemicals aside so that he could put them back on the shelf. He was careful to clean up his mess so that no one would come in contact with the sulfuric acid and burn their skin. When he was done cleaning up the area, he grabbed the ladder and leaned it up against the same shelf where he had stored the chemicals overnight. Roy was so happy that he was right that he wasn't paying full attention to what he was doing.

He grabbed the first bottles of chemicals to put away and climbed up the ladder. He reached up with his hand and placed them carefully on the shelf. Then he climbed down the ladder to get the others. His second trip up the ladder was just as easy. But what Roy didn't realize was that the ladder was slipping—just the tiniest bit—to one side. When he reached up to put the last of the chemicals on the shelf, the ladder slipped even more. Instead of putting the chemicals delicately on the shelf, his hand hit the shelf. Meanwhile, the ladder started falling to the floor. Roy looked up, but the chemicals weren't properly placed on the shelf. The shelf contents started to tip off the shelf and worse, the bottles were about to pour onto the front of Roy's head.

It was the sulfuric acid that spilled, the chemical that burns holes through concrete. It spilled onto his head, searing and burning through his skin into his flesh. He screamed for help, but no one was at home. The sulfuric acid poured down his head and onto his shoulders, burning flesh every inch of the way. It continued to run off of his shoulders and onto his chest and down his back. He fell to the floor and lifted his head. This is when the sulfuric acid started pouring down his forehead and spilled into his eyes. Roy continued to scream and tried to open his eyes so that he could run into the house and flush the chemicals out of his eyes and off of his skin, but every time he tried to open his eyes, the more the sulfuric acid burned. It was so painful that he could barely get off the floor.

His screams were finally heard by a neighbor, who called an ambulance. When the ambulance finally arrived, Roy was taken to the hospital. But it was too late; nothing could be done for his sight. The sulfuric acid had burned his eyes and taken his vision. He proved his instructor wrong, but at what cost? He would never see again.

Roy had made a lot of mistakes in his life, just like everyone else does, but this last one cost him his sight. The accident left him with emotional scars that were mightier than the physical ones. The physical ones would heal, but the emotional scars and guilt of having created the situation would last a lifetime. The next two to three months were painful, both emotionally and physically. He had to deal with the fact that he had caused his own blindness and that he was never going to see again, but he also had to deal with the physical pain and medical procedures that followed.

Roy had to undergo days and days of excruciatingly painful scraping of his wounds. Doctors needed to remove the burned and damaged skin and flesh so the healthy tissue was exposed and could grow and heal. Each time his burns were scraped, he was given morphine, but the morphine wasn't strong enough to hold back all of the pain. They also put him in water baths to try to sooth the wounds, but little of what they did alleviated the pain, which lasted for days on end after each treatment.

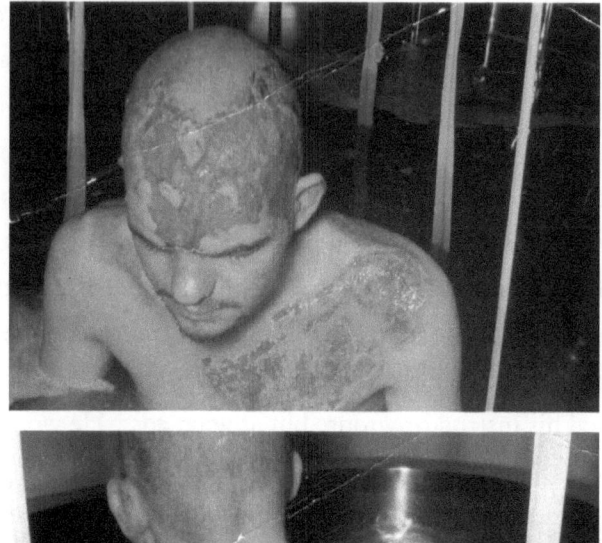
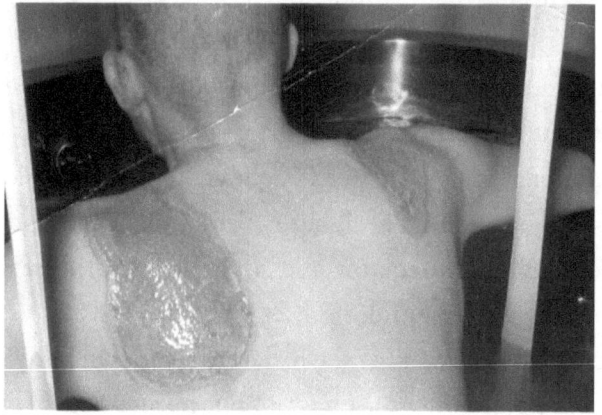

Figure 5: Roy in his soothing water baths after they had scraped his burns.

The excruciating pain and intense tightening of his skin during that recovery phase felt like it lasted a lifetime, but after approximately four months, the pain subsided and the wounds were starting to heal. Even though the wounds were not totally healed, Roy was pretty much pulled from the hospital burn treatment and pushed to go to the blind school. He didn't have much choice in the matter, and he really didn't have much time to find his own way after the accident or time to think about his life situation. Ironically, that's exactly why the doctors made him go to the blind school so that he could be around other blind people, and not have time to think about his choices.

During this transition, Roy quit school and lost his job. The one person he had relied on in his life and who he needed the most during this time of intense grief and change was his fiancée. Sadly, her sentiments weren't the same. A few days before Roy was supposed to go to the blind school, his fiancée told him she didn't want to see him again, and that he was on his own now. She said she did not want to be married to a blind man, and she walked out of Roy's life forever.

Roy was emotionally numb from all that he had just been through. He didn't know what to do now or what his future held, and his life seemed bleak. This definitely wasn't the life that he had planned for himself, and it wasn't what he had so excitedly envisioned just weeks before. He was now in total darkness, everything seemingly lost. He couldn't even fathom what his future might hold.

Chapter 3
Little Miss Independent—
Before I Knew Her as Mom

Diane was born with Primary Congenital Glaucoma (PCG), and has been pretty much blind since birth. PCG causes a buildup of pressure in the eyes that eventually chokes out and damages the optic nerve. Eyes contain fluid, and our bodies are constantly making and replacing this fluid. Normally, the fluid drains out of the eyes through cells and tissues, but in people with PCG, the fluid does not drain properly. It backs up, causing fluid pressure to build up. The pressure increases, together with the excess fluid itself, damaging the fibers of the optic nerve, which sends the signals to our brain so that we can see. Damage from PCG occurs slowly, but by the time it is noticed in an infant, the damage is usually extensive. By the time it was apparent something was wrong with Diane's eyes, the damage had already been done, and most of her vision was gone. There was nothing the doctors could do to bring it back.

Because of her PCG, Diane needed several surgeries during her childhood. In this way, the pressure in her eyes could be relieved, but because the surgeries were just temporary fixes, she had to have the pressure relieved several times. Recovery from the surgeries was very hard and painful for Diane, and she cried every time she had to have another one. She was a little girl fed up with all the pain and discomfort, and at one point screamed at the doctor removing her bandages, "I hate you!"

The very last surgery she had was when she was about 11 years old, and this last surgery caused further damage to her sight. The doctors removed the bandages and found that Diane's eyes had become severely infected. When the bandages were removed, there was no sight remaining at all. Diane's vision was total darkness. The doctor gave her weeks and weeks of antibiotic injections and eye drops trying to get rid of the infection. Once the infection was gone, a tiny bit of her vision came back a few weeks later, but her vision was far less than it had been before the surgery. The doctors told her that she had less than 10 percent of normal vision.

Diane's vision was such that she was able to discern the difference between light and dark objects. She could tell if it was daytime or nighttime. She could see if a lamp was on in the house at night. She could see that a person was standing in front of her in the daytime, and sometimes she could see faint bits of color, if the color was bright enough. She basically could only see big contrasts between objects, or enough to make out blurry objects. She could see enough to make out people, animals, and cars if the backgrounds behind them were a much different color. This tiny bit of vision that came back was what Diane was left to live with for the rest of her life.

· · · · · ·

Diane was born in 1939 in Aberdeen, South Dakota, during the aftermath of The Great Depression. Diane's parents had only eighth-grade educations, which meant good jobs were hard to come by, causing a lot of financial struggles for the family. Diane's family was poor, and they were just trying to make ends meet, like a lot of other families during this time.

Diane was the younger of two girls born to Ione and Elart. Her sister, Shirley, was four years older. Diane and Shirley's dad, Elart, was 19 years older than her mother, Ione. After the girls were born, Ione stayed home to raise the girls, and Elart worked odd jobs to support the family. Diane thought the world of her dad and was daddy's little girl. She always rushed to greet him at the door when he returned from work, and wanted to be by his side the rest of the evening. Elart bought Diane a baby buggy she had been begging him for on her fourth birthday. She was so happy when she opened the baby buggy. Diane put her dolls in the buggy, covered them up, and pushed them around all day long. Everywhere Diane went, she pushed her new baby buggy.

A few weeks after her birthday, her father kissed her goodbye and left for work as he normally did. She waited for him to come home, but he didn't. Diane never again saw or had any contact with her father after that. A few days after Elart left, Elart's brother, Woodrow, showed up at the house to help Ione with the two girls. Woody, as he was known, was the same age as Ione, and he adored Diane and her sister. Diane and Shirley knew Uncle Woody because he used to visit a lot, so he was no stranger coming into the house.

To Diane, it seemed that her father walked out and Woody just stepped right in to help take care of them. But that is the perception through the eyes of a child, and everything really wasn't what it seemed back then, although that may have been the story as told to two little girls who were only four and eight. All Diane or her sister knew is that when either of them mentioned their father, Elart, Woody and Ione would hush them and tell them not to talk about him. So eventually, the girls stopped mentioning their dad, and life went on as though his disappearance never happened.

Diane started to call Woody "Daddy," and both Diane and Shirley stopped mentioning Elart around the house. What really happened that year was kept secret for over 60 years. Woody and Ione had been having an affair. Woody would sneak over when Elart left for work, and sneak out before he came home. The affair started to get serious, and Ione kicked Elart out of the house so Woody could move in. The horrible thing is that Diane and Shirley were told that Elart was a no-good alcoholic who had just walked out of the house one day and decided he never wanted to come back. When Elart was told the news, he sadly left without putting up a fight, and without saying goodbye to his daughters. Elart had actually tried to see and visit his girls, but Ione and Woody never let him. Ione and Woody got married sometime after Elart left, and together they started raising Diane and Shirley as if nothing unusual had ever happened.

Diane was like any other little four-year-old in most every way. She was happy-go-lucky and rambunctious, with lots and lots of energy. She would run around the house playing with her sister Shirley when they had to stay inside. She loved to play house with her baby dolls and the baby buggy her father had bought for her. One day, Diane and Shirley were playing inside. Shirley was chasing Diane around the house, and Diane ran into the bathroom to get away. The color of the sink was the same color as the walls, and Diane couldn't see that very well, especially when she wasn't paying attention. In her fast escape into the bathroom, Diane had rammed her eye into the corner of the sink. She hit the sink so hard that it pushed her eye into her head, and permanently disfigured it.

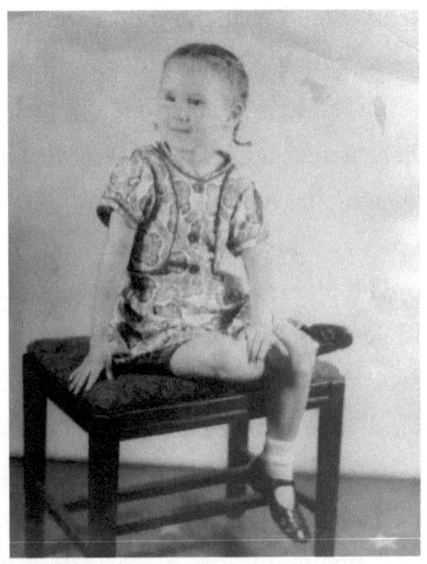

Figure 6: Diane at approximately five years old. This picture was taken after the injury to her eye. You can tell that her eye is pushed back a little farther than the other.

When Diane played outside, you could always find her playing with her sister, or maybe her best friend, Cecilia, who was sighted and the same age as Diane. Cecilia lived in the same apartment complex as Diane, so they were never far apart. Their parents would get together to play cards at night and on the weekends. While the adults played cards and drank, they would leave the kids to just run around and do whatever they wanted, without much supervision at all. Because of this, Cecilia and Diane always seemed to get into lot of mischief.

The apartment where they lived was close to the train station, and the train station was always a source of fun for the both of them. Diane and Cecilia would hear the train coming and run down to the train station to look at all the "bums," as they were called back then, getting off of the train. These were the men that were "riding the rails," as Diane would say, looking for work and traveling lightly from place to place. The men would sneak onto the train so they didn't have to pay, and sneak off when the trains stopped at a station so they could look for work. If the town didn't have any work, the men would get back on the next train, and ride it to the next destination. It was always fun to watch the strangers milling around the train station. Diane and Cecilia would stay and watch the men until they were bored and then would head back home.

They would pass the grocery store on their way back from the train station and frequently get into a little mischief there, too. They would bang on the metal sign in front of the grocery store, and run around the corner, lurking there to listen to the owner scream and try to find the kids that did it. They would laugh and wait for the owner to go back inside, then they would head back home like nothing ever happened. It was how two little girls had fun when there wasn't much else to do. Cecilia and Diane were inseparable. Even though they lived next door to each other, they would spend the night at each other's houses as much as they could.

One of the places Diane would go, knowing she had to behave, was the drug store on the other side of town. That's where she went with her mother to buy the medication needed for her eyes. The owner of the drug store was always nice and friendly to Diane, giving her ice cream or candy, and sometimes even a new toy to take home. She loved going there. Woody and Ione didn't have much money, and the owner of the drug store knew that and felt sorry for the little blind girl. On one of the visits to pick up Diane's eye medication, it was cold and snowy outside. Diane's winter coat had become too small to button up. The drug store owner noticed that Diane was too big for her coat, and told her to go pick out a pretty new winter coat to take home for free.

Diane started kindergarten the next year with her brand new winter coat. She attended the local school with all the other kids from her neighborhood. She was so excited to go to school and wanted to be just like all the other kids. She colored and painted pictures for her mom and new dad, and eagerly participated in all the indoor and outdoor activities, just like all the other kids. The other kids knew she was blind but treated her well, sometimes even helping her when she couldn't find what she was looking for. Diane was comfortable with all the other kids from her neighborhood and loved going to school with them. Kindergarten came and went without too much turmoil or complications, and she had no real difficulty dealing with her blindness. Her kindergarten experience at the local school was just like all other kindergarteners, and she was happy to be just like the other kids.

First grade was a different experience. Instead of laughing and coloring and playing around, first grade tasks were serious. The teachers were starting to teach the kids to read and write, and would write all the lessons on the chalkboard at the front of the classroom. Diane had trouble seeing the writing on the chalkboard, so her teachers moved her to the front row. Even after moving to the front of the class, though, she still couldn't see the writing on the board. It was too small, and there wasn't enough contrast. She sat in her class for the next six months, falling farther and farther behind, as she was simply unable to keep up with the other kids. So Woody and Ione made arrangements for her to attend the South Dakota School for the Blind. The school was located in Gary, South Dakota, over 150 miles away from where the family lived in Aberdeen. Diane would have to go there and stay without any of her family and friends. One day, Woody, Ione, and Shirley drove off to Gary, and Diane was dropped off to start her new school, all alone. This would be where Diane lived and went to school for the next eight years of her life, only coming home for summers and Christmas holidays.

The school had a total of 30 other blind students of all ages, who had come from all over South Dakota. They put all the students into different classes by age, and Diane's class only had three students. She would spend her days in the classroom with the other students. At night, she lived in a dorm-type room of her own in the girls' dormitory, where a house mom was always present. Diane attended classes just like any regular school, but her classes were taught by both sighted and blind teachers. The students were taught the same academic subjects of history, math, and English that any student of that age had to learn. All the blind children also attended gym class. The school had a regular gym and an outdoor area with a running track. In the warmer months, the girls would have to run the track for exercise.

The school track was lined with a horizontal bar the students could hold onto, and the students were also tethered to a pole alongside the bar to keep them in line as they ran. They girls also played a form of softball, using their arms to bat at a very soft ball, and even learned how to roller skate in the gym. In the wintertime, they would go ice skate on the pond at the school. The girls learned how to crochet, and were sometimes allowed to help cook. The boys had a wrestling team that travelled to other schools to compete. All 30 blind students would get on a bus and travel to the wrestling meets to support their school. They were a family of sorts.

On the weekends, the students would go downtown to walk around and shop, if they had money. In the evenings, the school had movies and events for the kids. There was also an apple orchard on campus where the students could climb trees and play hide and seek. Sometimes the boys would catch a snake out in the orchard and chase the girls around hanging on to it. The school also had a chorus and would hold concerts for the students and for the public to attend. Every once in a while, Diane's family would come for a visit, but it was never very often because they lived so far away. Mostly, Diane would talk to her family on the phone.

Whenever Diane had a phone call, she was called down to the office to talk. It was always her mom or sister on the phone, telling her all the great news that was going on with her friends and family. When Ione was pregnant, they called Diane to tell her that she was going to have a little brother or sister soon. A few months later, her little sister, Linda, was born. They put the phone up to little Linda's ear, and let Diane talk to her and say hello. When Ione was pregnant for the second time, they called Diane to tell her that her new baby brother had arrived. Ione and Woody even let Diane pick out her new little brother's name from the several they were considering. Diane decided Larry would be her new little brother's name.

Other times she was called down to the office because she had received a care package. The nice drug store owner from Aberdeen, who had given Diane the free winter coat, would often send care packages filled with candy and treats. Diane wasn't allowed to take the package back to her room, though. All the candy had to be monitored, so once she opened it, she had to give it over to the house mom. Each night after dinner, Diane could take one or two candies back to her room. Diane always suspected that the house mom was eating her candy and stealing things from the box, because when she went back home, the drug store owner asked if she got the package and mentioned some of the things—never received—that he had sent to her.

Figure 7: Female students at the South Dakota School for the Blind. Diane is the one sitting at the bottom of the teeter-totter.

The first time Diane came home for the summer, she was just six years old, and her sister was 10. It was all fun and games that summer, and Diane spent plenty of time playing with her best friend, Cecilia. When Cecilia wasn't around, Diane tried to join her sister and her sister's friends, but Shirley didn't want anything to do with Diane. Shirley would tell Diane to close her eyes and count to ten, and when Diane was done counting and opened her eyes, Shirley and her friends were nowhere to be found. The second summer home was pretty much the same, but by then, Ione was pregnant with their baby sister.

As time went on and the family started to grow, the more responsibility was piled onto Shirley to take care of her younger siblings. Diane started to help take care of her younger siblings, too, at least when she came home for the summers, even though she was only eight years old. She started taking care of Linda because Ione and Woody were off at work trying to make ends meet. Summers weren't all fun and play anymore, because now she had to stay in and help take care of her siblings. Whenever Ione wasn't working, she was playing cards with her friends, leaving the kids to run around as they pleased. Either Shirley or Diane watched after the younger kids, and the two older girls did most of the housework. Ione would always say "I had you kids so I don't have to do the work around here!"

As they got older, Shirley would leave it to Diane, preferring to spend more and more time with her boyfriend away from her family. Eventually, Shirley left the house at 16 years old, when she got pregnant. Shirley married her boyfriend, Joe, and they left for California to live with Joe's sister and husband.

Figure 8: Shirley and Joe on their wedding day

For three years, Shirley wrote letters back home telling everyone how wonderful California was and how much Joe was working. Woody and Ione were finding it harder and harder to find work, so in 1955, when Diane was just about 15 years old, Woody drove out to California to search for work. Woody soon found work, and the whole family moved to California. Diane had to leave the South Dakota School for the Blind before she was finished, so that she could move with her growing family. Diane left school early to help Ione sell all of their belongings and pack up the kids for the train ride from South Dakota to Los Angeles, California.

It was a long train ride that lasted for several days, but it seemed even longer with all the kids. By this time, Ione and Woody had four kids of their own. Ione was pregnant for the trip to California. Diane was 15 years old, Linda was seven, Larry was six, Nancy was three, and youngest child, Rick, was just a few months old. The train ride was long, stopping at most every town along the way toward California. When they got to California, Joe and Shirley met them at the Los Angeles train station and drove them to Huntington Beach, CA, where Woody had rented a gas station where all of them could live. Woody hosed out one of the stalls, and thought it was a good place for everyone to live because it was cheap until they could get on their feet. But Ione refused to live in the gas station stall with all the children, and looked for a place close to where Shirley and Joe lived. The next day, they moved into a two-bedroom, one-bath house very close to Shirley and Joe.

Rick slept in a crib in Ione and Woody's bedroom, while Linda, Larry, and Nancy shared the second bedroom. Diane didn't have a room and slept on a sofa that folded into a bed. Diane only had to live that way for a few months, because shortly after coming to California, she left for the California School for the Blind (CSB) in Berkeley, California. Woody, Ione, and the kids drove for almost eight hours to drop her off at her new school. The trip to CSB was a full day's drive from where they lived in Southern California, and Diane arrived to the school exhausted. Woody, Ione, and the kids drove back that same day. Shortly after Diane went back to school, another new baby brother was born.

Diane was 16 years old when she started going to the California School for the Blind (CSB). It was the same kind of school as the one in Gary, but so much bigger. The school taught grade K-9, and since Diane was behind in school by then, she attended the 9th grade when she was 16 years old. She lived at CSB for another two years, along with several other high school students, before switching to Berkeley High School. All the blind girls attended

Berkeley High School, and all the blind boys attended Oakland Tech High School, even though they all lived at CSB. Diane would get up in the morning and ride the bus to Berkeley High School, then ride the bus back to the CSB. In the evenings, the students who attended high school would have to go to a study hall in the evenings. The study hall employed state-paid readers who would come in the evening to read school assignments and help them do their homework.

When Diane first arrived at the blind school, she didn't fit in. She was behind in school, for one thing, and quite a bit older than the other students in the same grade. Worse, she also just came from South Dakota and wasn't like all the other kids. She was teased a lot and called a "hick." Her parents were really poor when she first came to California, so she didn't have any new school clothes, either. The boys were mean to her. They would tell her, "Close your eyes and open your hands. I have a surprise for you." Then they would somehow put a bee in her hand. When she felt to see what they had given her, she would get stung. So life at CSB was a little rough in the beginning, but eventually settled down when she started making friends.

She attended CSB during the school year and would take the train home for Christmas holidays and summers. There were several students whose families lived in Southern California, so they would all ride in one train car with a chaperone. It was an all-day trip on the train, but was fun riding back with all her schoolmates.

After finishing 9th and 10th grade, and living at the California School for the Blind in Berkeley, Diane moved back to live with her family and attended the next couple years at a Garden Grove High School, a regular high school that had mostly sighted students. At

Garden Grove High School, there was a person enlisted to walk her to each of her classes. She had state-paid readers that would read her the daily assignments. The reader would also take her to lunch, and show her to the bus when school was over. The bus would pick her up and drop her off in the driveway of her home, so she never had the chance to get lost.

Diane graduated from high school in May of 1958, but had to wait a full year before a slot would come open for her to attend Orientation Center for the Blind (OCB). She left for OCB in 1959, when she was 19 years old.

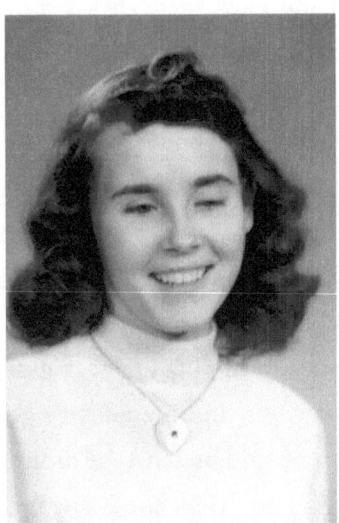

Figure 9: Diane's high school graduation picture.
She graduated Garden Grove High School
in California in 1958.

During this year when she was home, she was in charge of watching after her younger brother and sisters. She had a really good relationship with her younger siblings, even though she was away at school for most of their lives. Since Ione and Woody were both working to support the family, Diane was the primary one taking care of the household. She would wake up in the morning and give her youngest brother Randy a bottle, then do the laundry and hang it out to dry. In the afternoons, she would take the laundry off the line, fold it, and put it away. She would make lunch for the kids and make sure they were behaving throughout the day.

Most of the time, Diane would make all the kids stay inside because they were easier to take care of that way. But Linda and Larry were older, and always wanted to go outside to play with their friends. Linda and Larry were always trying to come up with ingenious ways to trick their blind sister into letting them outside. Larry would sneak outside and ring the doorbell. When Diane answered the door, Larry would pretend to be someone else, and ask for Larry to be able to come out and play. Sometimes Larry would knock on the door from the inside, and try to sneak out and pretend he had always been outside. Diane was always aware of all the tricks, and would chase them inside the house. They would hide under the bed to get away, hoping Diane couldn't notice them. But Diane was older and wiser, and pretended right along with them. She would take a broom and pretend she didn't see them under the bed, just like they wanted. Then she'd whack under the bed with a broom, "cleaning dust," until they couldn't take it anymore and screamed for her to stop.

Although the year home taking care of her siblings was hectic, she was finally able to get to know her younger brothers and sisters. This year helped forge the close relationship she has with them all.

As I Saw It

Figure 10: Ione and Woody's children from left to right.
Top: Linda, Larry; Bottom: Nancy, Randy, and Ricky

Chapter 4
Life at Blind School

I WASN'T AWARE OF EVERYTHING MY PARENTS needed to learn in order to live a life on their own. I just thought they learned what they needed automatically, or they picked up how to do things from their parents—because that's how I learned.

Diane's parents didn't know exactly how to teach or show her how to do things from a blind perspective. Her parents relied on their sight for almost everything that they did, and they didn't know how to show Diane how to do things relying on her other senses. They also didn't know everything that Diane needed to know. It's very hard for a sighted person to try to show a blind person how to do something, because they always try to show them from their own sighted perspective, which usually doesn't work very well. That's why most blind persons need to go to a blind school where specialized life skills are taught, so they can learn how to do things independently from a blind person's perspective.

Diane and Roy wouldn't have been to make it on their own if it wasn't for the training they received at the Occupational Center for the Blind (OCB) in Berkeley, California. This is the place that changed both of their lives forever. It is the place where they met, but it is also the place where they learned how to live on their own, how to travel by themselves, and how to handle the many different things that came up in their lives. Our family wouldn't have existed without it, let alone been successful.

Diane and Roy both came to OCB in 1960, although they started at different times of the year. There were approximately 30 students attending there at the time, each of them had varying backgrounds and all had different levels of blindness. Some of the students couldn't see anything but darkness, like Roy, and others had a little bit of limited sight, like Diane. But they were all there for the same reason. They had all relied on sighted people for pretty much everything in their life, and now they were all ready to learn how to do it on their own. Yes, they were scared. And yes, it was a pretty confusing time for them, especially for Roy. After all, he had just gone blind a few months prior, and the major focus in his life immediately afterward had been healing from his burns. He really hadn't had time to try to adjust to his blindness. But he wasn't the first one there under similar circumstances. Everyone was different, and they all had unique stories and different needs. But that's what was great about this school. It helped everyone who was blind, and they at least had that major need in common. It was a place that reassured them that they would be able to do it all on their own and everything would come together for them.

Diane and Roy, as well as their lifelong friend, Josie, have told me countless stories about going to OCB and what a wonderful experience they had. They told me how confusing it was when they first arrived and what stood out at first was how different everyone's needs were. Diane and Josie were both born blind and had been getting around for the most part by themselves without too much help for their whole lives. They were both still relying on sighted people for guidance, but felt comfortable being alone in their houses, for example. There were also people who had just gone blind suddenly, like Roy, who used to rely on their sight and perhaps only had a few weeks or months to adjust to their new blindness. The school was great for everyone because it always met them where they were, devising plans to help them according to their immediate needs.

Diane told me that when she first arrived, she was taken to her dorm room and guided around her room so that she knew where everything was. School staff were present to help the students with most everything, and answer all their questions, in the beginning. They were escorted wherever they needed to go, and given as much help as they needed, until they were comfortable in their new surroundings. They were escorted to and from the cafeteria for meals by a sighted person, along with several other blind students who had been at the school for a while. Diane would grab the sighted person's arm, and the other blind students would walk by themselves following along. They all walked together in a group so they could all talk and get to know each other. The school had a very friendly atmosphere, and encouraged students to get to know one another. That's another reason why most everything was done in teams or groups.

The first goal was to get the students able to start doing things on their own, so one of the first things they learned was how to effectively use a cane. They were shown how to hold the cane, how to maneuver it, and then how to start walking with it. As Diane explained to me, "We were taught to tap our cane on the right, then sweep it to the left, then tap on the left and sweep it to the right, all while taking a few steps forward."

When a sighted person walks, he or she looks to maneuver around obstacles, to know when the surfaces change or are uneven, and when there are steps. But what happens to a sighted person when he/she isn't paying attention? A sighted person bumps into things, they stumble because they accidentally stepped off the sidewalk and into the grass, or they trip because there was a lip or gap in the concrete or some obstacle in their path. Walking, for a blind person, is similar at best to a sighted person who is walking without paying attention. Blind persons need to notice all of the obstacles, terrain differences, and surface differences, but they do it all by touch and sound, using their cane.

Tapping the cane provides a way to get feedback from sound, to be able to determine what type of surface and the texture of the surface, and swiping the cane across in front makes sure that the path ahead is clear of any obstacles and alerts a blind person to any differences. Once the students are familiar with their canes, they practice, practice, practice until they are comfortable. Then they start learning how to get to the cafeteria and back to their rooms on their own and start to learn how to get around campus to the different buildings so they can go to their classes on their own. It definitely wasn't easy at first. Diane and Josie would sometimes walk right off the sidewalk and into the grass, their canes would get caught in cracks and in between things, they'd bump into things, and once in a while even trip and fall down. Each of the students supported one another, and part of their learning was to get past all these little hurdles. They were all in it together, and they encouraged and helped each other.

They also had to learn other things they would need in their daily lives. Diane and Josie had both learned Braille at a young age, but there were some students at the school who had more recently became blind, like Roy, or some who had never been taught, and they needed to relearn how to read. For anyone who doesn't know, Braille is a way of reading and writing that can be interpreted by touch. Braille consists of arranged, raised dots on paper, so that the dots can be discerned by touch. Each letter and number is created using a Braille cell that consists of six dots—three dots high and two across.

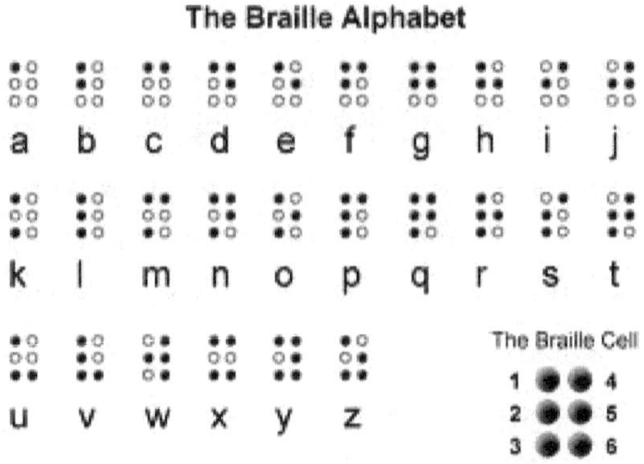

Figure 11: Braille Cell and Braille Alphabet

The young ladies were sometimes taught different skills than the young men. Diane and Josie learned how to iron. They started out ironing small things like a hankie, then they would iron bigger things like pillowcases, just so they could get used to moving the cloth around and making sure to iron the whole piece. They eventually moved on to clothing, learning how to iron collars and sleeves. They would iron a place on the material, let it cool a bit, feel where the wrinkles still were, and progress accordingly until they had finished the whole piece. They also learned how to sew so that they could mend their own clothes. They learned how to thread a needle using a needle threader, and learned a few different types of stitches so they would be able to mend a ripped seam, hem pants and skirts, and label their clothes. Back then, there were little metal tags that could be sewn onto clothing labels, so they knew what color their clothes were and if each item had stripes, polka dots, or prints. If their clothes were labeled, they wouldn't accidentally put together a striped blouse with plaid pants, or combine colors that didn't go together. The blind school taught them everything.

I was shocked by some of the things Diane and Josie were taught. Since Diane never wore anything other than lipstick, I didn't realize they were taught how to put on makeup. They were taught how to put on foundation, blush, eye shadow--pretty much the whole works. This is my conversation with Josie about learning to put on makeup at school:

Me: So what else did you guys learn at OCB?
Josie: Well, we learned how to apply makeup and—
Me: You mean they taught you how to put on makeup?
Josie: Yes.
Me: How did they do that?
Josie: They brought in a lady from the department store. She picked out colors for us and then showed us how to apply it—
Me: [Laughing]
Josie: —and then you had to apply it on your own, and the lady would come around and tell you what you did wrong and what to do differently. So we had to re-do it until we got it right.

Me: [Still laughing]

Josie: [A little flabbergasted from my laughing] Well, Laura, even sighted people put too much makeup on.

After learning how to read Braille, and once they were able to get around pretty well on their own, they were taught how to cook using Braille recipes. They would read their Braille recipe, and make out their shopping list. Then they would have to go to the grocery store to buy the groceries before they could actually cook. They were being taught how they were going to have to do it in real life. When they got back from the grocery store, the teacher would show them how to prepare. She would show them how to cut things up, and how to use measuring cups and spoons with special raised markings, which is how they could tell the different sizes apart. The teacher would explain how to make the recipes and then would walk around answering questions and showing them how to do it, checking to see if they needed any help.

They had to learn everything they would need in all aspects of their lives, from what they needed to learn to have a successful household, to what they needed for all the business type transactions they might encounter. That's why all the students were taught how to sign their names. Learning how to sign her name wasn't easy for Diane. Diane might have seen print a couple of times when she was little, but being blind, she might not have been able to decipher individual letters unless it was very large print. So she pretty much didn't know what printed lettering was, and that's what made learning how to sign her name that much harder. She never learned to write or read in the sighted way as a little girl. I mean, she could say her alphabet like all the other children, but blind people just weren't taught to write. Roy, on the other hand, had been sighted as a child, and he had been signing his name for years before he lost his sight. So he really didn't have to learn how to sign his name, but Diane and many of the other students that were born blind needed to learn.

The only letters she had really learned were Braille letters, and printed letters are a whole lot different. Diane had to learn how to write the alphabet first, just like any other kid learns in grade school, except she was a grown adult by this time. When she first learned how to sign her name, she had to practice and practice just like every other person has to, but she couldn't see to get direct feedback on how to improve it. I know that my handwriting evolved over time—lots of time. But that's because I was always able to see it and then change it as I wanted. But when Diane learned to sign her name, it pretty much stayed the same over time. So imagine if you still handwrote like you had learned in third grade. Well, that's what Diane's signature looks like, even as an older adult. She learned it once, mastered it, and it has never changed since.

Figure 12: Diane's Signature

Figure 13: Roy's Signature

As I Saw It

Figure 14: Blind friends at Occupational Center for the Blind in Berkeley, CA. Diane is in the center right with her dress laid out. Josie is in the center to the left.

They were all just typical students at OCB, college-aged and all, and sometimes they didn't feel like going to class. Some of them would hide out in their dorm rooms instead of going to class. Roy was notorious for trying to skip class. The first couple of times he stayed in his room and didn't go to class, good ole' Pete, the mobility instructor, wouldn't let him get away with it. If Roy didn't show up for Pete's mobility lesson, Pete would go to the office and get the key to his room. Pete would walk in and wait until Roy got dressed and then escort him to class. Pete didn't let them get away with very much at all.

It wasn't just Roy who tried to get out of going to classes; everyone tried to get away with things. When the students had to go off campus for their mobility assignments, sometimes they would all meet up at a coffee shop instead of walking around town doing their assignment for the day. Yes, Pete was onto them then, too. He would drive around in the area where they were supposed to be walking, looking for them. If he couldn't find them, he'd go into all the different cafes and stores until he found the group, and get them walking around like they were supposed to.

Things weren't always so serious. The students had the evenings and weekends all to themselves. In the evenings after classes, they would hang out in different groups with the friends they had met. Diane and Josie were always together, and did most everything together. Sometimes a small group of them would go off campus to a diner and to get something to eat and socialize.

Saturdays were "date" nights. Josie was dating another student named Ron, and Diane and Roy started dating shortly after he got out of the hospital. The four of them were always doing things together. They would sometimes just hang out at a diner or go to a movie or bowling. Roy was good at convincing everyone to go out. They'd catch a bus to the movie theater, buy their tickets, and all find a seat close to the aisle. Someone sitting down would stick their cane into the aisle, and Roy would go buy popcorn and drinks. He carried everything in one hand, and walk down the aisle with his cane until his cane hit the cane sticking into the aisle. That's how he'd know which seats to bring the popcorn and drinks back to.

Going to OCB was just like any other college-type experience. The students went to classes, learned what they needed to, but also went out and had fun, as normal young adults. They met wonderful friends who they still keep in touch with today. OCB was a very positive experience for all of them. OCB gave them more than just training to become independent adults; it was the special place that gave them the courage and confidence to live on their own at a time when society didn't think they could.

"After going to OCB, you knew that life would go on and you could make it on your own and live a normal life like anybody else."
–Josie, Diane and Roy's lifelong friend

Chapter 5
Just Starting Out—
Making New Lives Together

MY MOM AND DAD GOT MARRIED ON November 30, 1961 in Oakland, California, and they honeymooned for two weeks in Lake Tahoe. Roy's mom, Ellon, traveled in for the wedding, but the relationship between Roy and his siblings was still a little strained. None of his siblings came to the wedding. Diane's mom, Ione, and dad, Woody, came, but the younger kids stayed home because they were all still in school. All of Roy and Diane's blind friends they had met at blind school came, and even some of the people that Roy had worked with back at the cement factory all came to their wedding.

Their wedding was pretty traditional. They got married in a small church and afterwards they had a simple reception with cake and presents. It was a happy time. It is hard to believe that one fateful day at the blind school, when Pete the mobility instructor gave my mom and Josie their assignment, offering companionship after my dad's horrible hit-and-run accident, led to this and changed their lives forever. And now they were getting ready to start their lives together.

Figure 15: Wedding Day. Left to right: Ellon (Roy's mom), Diane, Roy, Ione (Diane's mom), and Woody (Diane's "dad")

Figure 16: Their reception

When Diane and Roy got back from their honeymoon, they lived in the small apartment that Diane had been living in after she left the blind school, waiting for Roy to get out. They only spent a short time there, as they soon found a place to call their own. They moved to the upstairs apartment of a house owned by an elderly lady. It was close to where they had been living, near bus stops and, in general, a good neighborhood that was easy for them to get around. Family and friends helped them move. After only a few short weeks of living in their new apartment, Diane broke the news to Roy: she was pregnant, and they were going to be parents. They were excited with the thought of being parents, but the elderly lady who owned the house wasn't. She did not want children in her house, and told Diane and Roy that they could not live there with a baby. So my parents had to search for another place to live again before I was born. They found another cozy apartment close by, and I was born—just a short nine and a half months after they were married.

Figure 17: My mom and me

Figure 18: My dad and me (4 months old)

Having a new baby to take care of is stressful enough, but shortly after I was born, my parents' life together got pretty tough. It wasn't because of having me to take care of me; it was because tragedy number three for my dad was starting. My dad started to get excruciating pain in the leg that had been broken in the hit-and-run accident. He had consistently had trouble with his leg after the accident, and had to wear a leg brace. He had walked with a limp since the accident, but started to develop pain, and the pain progressed quickly to being unbearable. My dad's pain was so bad that after a few days, the pain medication wasn't helping at all. He could barely move his leg. He couldn't sleep, as the pain was too great, no matter how he positioned his leg. He finally couldn't take it anymore, so the family doctor he had been seeing referred him to an orthopedic specialist to find out what was wrong.

The orthopedic specialist examined his leg and sent him directly to the hospital for some tests and bloodwork. Thank goodness he went to the hospital right away, because the hospital found that my dad had developed gangrene in his leg, meaning it was starting to rot and the tissue around the broken bone was starting to die. The doctor didn't know the extent of the damage, though, and surgery was indicated either way. So when he broke the news to my dad, he said, "I cannot tell the extent of the damage to your leg, so I can't say for sure if I'll be able to save it. I won't know until I can open you up and take a look inside."

The news after surgery wasn't great news to my mom. But my mom and dad were thankful that the doctor was able to save his leg. The gangrene had just started and did not affect blood flow to the area of his leg so badly that he needed to get his leg amputated. But the damage to his leg was pretty severe. Several doctors performed the actual surgery, in which they had to remove one of his ribs to replace the bone that had been damaged, and also had to remove skin from other parts of his body to graft to the wound on his leg so that it would heal properly. The first thing my dad did after waking up from surgery was reach down to feel if his leg was still there. There was nothing else in the world that mattered except the feeling of knowing that his leg was still there. Recovery wasn't easy, and my dad had to stay in the hospital for quite a while before they let him come home.

While my dad was at the hospital recovering, my mother was left at home by herself to take care of me when I was just a few days old. My dad was finally released from the hospital almost a month after surgery, but he still had a long and painful journey ahead of him to get back on his feet. So for the next six weeks, my mom had to take care of a newborn *and* my dad. None of their family or friends were able to come help out in the beginning, so they had to wait until my grandmother Ellon, my dad's mom, was finally able to come help them out for a couple of months until my dad could get around a little on his own. My mom and dad's first year together was definitely full of surprises. Thank goodness things settled down and they were finally able to start to make plans for their future again.

My mom and dad's marriage was pretty traditional for a marriage back in the early 1960s. My mom took care of cleaning the house, cooking dinner, and taking care of me—and that was fine with my mom. She loved being a mother and a housewife, as she was called back then. My dad didn't work because he was considered disabled because of his blindness. Yet he didn't want to collect disability, social security, or whatever other public assistance he qualified for forever. For a while he was kind of stuck until he could get around on his leg a little better. He used this time of healing to figure out what he wanted to do with his life, and to slowly start to do things as he was able.

My dad had always been interested in ham radios, at least since he moved out to California. He used to go out to the airfield and watch the planes and ham radio operators before he went blind. Most of the guys at the airfield were ham radio operators, too. My dad would watch them talk on their radios. He would ask them loads of questions, and they would teach him all about ham radios and how they worked, and told him that he should get his license. My dad talked and fiddled with their ham radios and vowed to get one of his own sometime. Ever since his visits to the airfield before he went blind, getting his license and a ham radio had been on his mind. So while he was recovering from his leg surgery, he taught himself Morse code, a requirement for getting his ham radio license back then.

When he was able to get around a little bit on his leg, he also joined the local blind club and became as active as he could despite limitations with his leg. He became good friends with the current president of the blind club, who would come to our house pretty regularly. Together, they would spend hours drafting and writing legislation for blind rights. My dad got very involved in blind and disabled rights, and later fought for equal rights for the disabled through his participation in the blind club.

When my dad's leg started to get better, he decided that he wanted to go back to school so he could get a job and take care of his family. He didn't want to go back to school for chemistry, though. This time, he wanted to make a difference in people's lives, especially others like him who had been in tragic accidents and were having trouble figuring it all out and getting back on their feet. He signed up for classes at a local community college. After a semester or so, he decided he wanted to go into rehabilitation counseling and become a rehabilitation counselor. What this meant, though, was many, many years of going to school and lots of hard work. My dad was up for the challenge, and my mom supported and encouraged him to follow his dreams.

My dad was gone pretty much all day taking classes, doing homework, and studying, just like he would have been gone if he had a job, while my mom was home taking care of the house, cooking, and taking care of me, and later, my brother. My mom really didn't have much help at all. She kept the house cleaned and vacuumed so that I couldn't find anything to put in my mouth. She cooked dinner every night and cleaned up afterwards. She did what most every other housewife back in the 1960s did. My mom had a lady that would come once a week to help out around the house to clean, do laundry, or anything else my mom needed, and another lady that came once a month to make out the bills. My mom pretty much did all the rest herself, with some help and support from my dad, of course.

There was more service available for everyday tasks back then. My mom ordered groceries over the phone, and the local grocery store would deliver the groceries to her and the other housewives in the neighborhood. My mom had a lot of practice taking care of babies from taking care of her younger siblings as well as from the life skills she'd learned at OCB that made up the specialized training she needed to care for a home and family.

She was a careful mom. She put the phone inside a cabinet to muffle the sound, for example, in case someone tried to call when I was taking naps. If I was crying, she would methodically and carefully check the pins in my diaper to see if they were sticking me, make sure that I didn't have a dirty diaper, and then make sure I wasn't hungry. If she couldn't find anything wrong, but she felt something wasn't right, or an accident happened—like the time she broke a glass on the kitchen floor and I crawled into the kitchen before she cleaned it up—she'd scoop me up in her arms and carry me over to a neighbor's house so they could reassure my mom that everything looked okay. She just wanted a sighted person's reassurance that there was nothing visibly wrong to make sure that she hadn't missed anything.

When I got a little older, though, my mom was always running over to the neighbor's house with me in her arms. As soon as I started to crawl, I started climbing. I'd climb on the counters, climb on dressers, climb all over the furniture, and anything else that I could. With all the climbing came a lot of falling, too. My mom said that she was always taking me to the emergency room in a taxi for something. It seems that every time I would fall, I'd fall onto my head and get a huge lump. I definitely was not the easiest child to take care of, and always kept my mom and dad on their toes.

Some of neighbors where we lived during that time were almost like family. The elderly couple across the street, who I called Nonnie and Papa, couldn't have any children of their own. My mom welcomed them with open arms and treated them like her own parents. Petrina and Johnny were their "real" names, and they loved having me over. They would always cook for me and give me loads of candy. We were just like a family. Nonnie and Papa would babysit me once in a while so that my mom and dad could go out, and sometimes I'd even spend the night with them. They were always there for my parents.

When my mom got pregnant again and my brother was born, four years after me, they took me over to Nonnie and Papa's house for a few days so that my mom could take care of my new little brother, David. Shortly after David was born, my dad was ready to transfer to a university, so we moved to an apartment with a playground and lots of other families with kids. From there, my dad would be closer to the college, and my brother and I could meet friends and have a place to play outside. Occasionally, Nonnie and Papa would come to visit, and my mom and dad kept in contact with them for many years. We all missed Nonnie and Papa, but at that time it really was necessary to move, so it was easier for my dad to catch a bus to get to his classes.

Figure 19: My mom, brother (2 years old), and me (6 years old)

My dad caught the bus just outside the apartment, in fact, and it took him directly to the college campus. He would get off the bus and walk to his classes by himself using his cane, at least after the first couple of times when someone showed him how to get there. Occasionally, he would be deep in thought about one of his classes, and make a wrong turn, but the other students were pretty helpful in getting him where he needed to go. My dad usually took the same bus at the same time, and the bus would always let him off at the same location on campus. Going home was routinized, too, with a set schedule.

One day, though, the bus couldn't get all the way onto campus because a group of picketers from the painters' union was protesting about the university using non-union painters to paint the Fine Arts Building. My dad was therefore dropped off at a different location, and couldn't find his way to his classes. Later, the busses were not at the regular location to catch them back home. One day he was trying to find his bus to go home, and he called out asking if anyone was around to help him. No one responded. He tried to go on his own, but fell down. He later learned that the picketers were just 20 feet away and saw him struggling the whole time. My dad is not a violent man, and would never hurt another person, but he was very angry and somewhat humiliated when he realized what had happened. The next day, he went over to one of the men picketing, and broke his sign in half. I found the letter that he sent to the editor of *The Pioneer*, the university newspaper, in response to the newspaper article about the broken picket sign. This is the letter is from May, 1969.

Editor:

This letter is in response to an article published May 3, p.3 regarding the incident in which "an amazing blind man" and two of his followers harassed a "friendly picket." It is unfortunate that the writer failed to seek the reason why the incident occurred. All of us students, for more than two weeks prior to this incident, had been late to our classes because the AC Transit bus could not cross the picket line. In my case, I was forced to ask, and later plead, and even beg some student on the bus to show me the way through the parking lot so that I could from that point find my own class.

Many students and some members of the faculty and the administration were not even aware that the AC bus was being blocked by the picketing.

Both of the AC bus drivers had at times violated the picket line on behalf of all students and in particular the handicapped. For this, they were firmly reprimanded by their own union.

The hardship caused me was not, however, the reason I so irrationally tore up the picket sign.

The day prior to this incident, I became lost, and a lady stopped and offered me a ride to where I could catch the bus. I asked her where she had picked me up in relation to the pickets, and what they were dong at the time. She replied, "Two of them were sitting in the shade about twenty feet away, pointing at you and laughing."

The next morning I asked, as always, for someone on the bus to show me the way through the parking lot. One student said that he was going to the library and would show me the way. As we stepped off the bus, I asked him to guide me over to the picket and tell me when we got there. I asked the picket the following questions: 1. "Does your union realize that what an ordeal it is causing students, handicapped or not, by blocking this bus?" The picket did not reply. 2. "Do you realize that in blocking this bus, you are hurting no one except students who are trying to get to class?" There was still no answer. 3. "Are you one of those pickets who yesterday laughed at me as I was falling down, lost and unable to find my way through the parking lot to this bus stop?" Again, there was no reply.

I reached out, not "groping," and broke the sign into pieces, saying, "When your union really understands what it has been doing to me personally, as well as to all students who must ride the bus, then they will know why this picket sign is broken."

I want to make one thing clear. It was I, and I alone, who broke that sign, and I did it because I am not "an amazing blind man." I am just one man who does not like to be laughed at.

Roy Phelps

While my dad was in school, my mom was busy taking care of us. Josie, her friend from the blind school, had two children also. Josie's older daughter, Anna, was two months younger than me, and Kelly was close in age to my brother. We would often go out together. Sometimes we'd just get out of the house to get something to eat or go shopping, but other times it was someplace fun. My mom and Josie were always surprising us and taking us to different places. They didn't want us to miss out on anything in life just because they were blind, so they made an effort to take us to lots of places. We went to the circus, parks, zoos, movies, amusement parks, and all the fairs and carnivals that came to town. Most of the time, the fun trips would be very long days, because we'd have to ride many buses to get there. There was always waiting for each of the buses in between, too. But that's how we got around as a family. As kids, my brother and I knew no difference. For us, and for Anna and Kelly, it was just normal.

Whenever we'd get to our destination, we'd take our moms by the arms and lead them around to whatever we wanted to do. At the fair, for example, my mom and Josie would wait for us next to the rides so we could grab their arms again to go to the next one. Our moms would stand by our side when we played the concession games too. Occasionally, they would ride the rides with us and play the games alongside us. At one of the fairs, the carnival person at the booth where darts are thrown at balloons to win prizes convinced our moms that it was super easy to win, and they could even do it being blind. So Josie and my mom gave it a try. The carnival guy gave them each a free dart to try and gave them a lesson how to hold the darts and how to throw them.

Both my mom and Josie threw the darts, and actually won us huge stuffed animals. Josie's daughters picked out a pink and white dog, and

I picked out a green and white bull. We were all jumping up and down happy as could be when our moms won. The carnival guy started yelling, "It's so easy to win. Look what these blind ladies just won."

All four of us kids were smiling ear to ear. What we didn't realize, though, is that we had to carry these big stuffed animals, at least three feet high, around the rest of the day. We carried our prizes around for a few hours until we couldn't take it anymore, and started crying because they were so awkward and heavy to carry. We had to leave the fair earlier than planned, and my mom and Josie ended up carrying these gigantic toys on all the buses we had to take to get back home. I still remember all the people on the bus staring at the prizes that our moms had won, and being amazed to learn that our blind moms had won them throwing darts at balloons.

When my mom wasn't taking us out, my brother and I were playing outside with the other kids that lived in our apartment complex. We did a lot more than play, though; sometimes we got into a lot of trouble. The apartment complex had an incinerator to burn trash. There was a distinct warning on it not to put aerosol cans into it. Of course, being the little mischievous kids that we were, we didn't care what the sign stated. We would dig through the trash cans and find all the aerosol cans we could, and then we'd toss them into the fire. We'd run around the corner and wait for the big boom! We weren't always getting into trouble, sometimes we just rode our bikes around and played hide and seek or cops and robbers with our neighborhood friends. We loved it outside and would beg to go out and play.

It was a whole different time back in the '60s and '70s. My parents didn't have to be worried about kidnapping and stranger danger as parents need to now. It was normal for parents to let their children roam the neighborhood in the company of others school-aged and up, and visit one another's houses or the local parks. One of their biggest worries, when my brother and I were little kids, was that we'd somehow wander away when we were outside playing—or that we'd somehow get separated from our parents or each other when we were out in public. Being blind, they couldn't go around looking for us, so their solution was to make us learn our address and phone number as soon as we started to talk. My mom and dad thought it was important to be able to tell someone who could help us find our way back. My parents always told us to ask for a police officer if we ever got lost so that we could tell him our address so he could bring us home. I was only a few years old when we moved to that apartment in Hayward, California, but our address was so engrained in my head back then, I can still remember it today: 27808 Manon Avenue, Apartment 20.

Even before my brother was born, my parents taught me enough about the bus system so I'd know what busses to take to get back home in case I was ever separated from them when we were away from home. My mother would test me sometimes when we were out shopping. She would ask me "How would you get home from here?" And I would recite back to her all the different busses I'd have to take to get back home. My mom would smile knowing that I knew how to make it back home by myself if I ever got lost, and I'd love all the positive attention that I got from being told how smart I was. My parents had to be creative and figure out ways to make up for not being able to see to keep my brother and me safe. Sometimes raising kids took a little ingenuity, but all in all it was the life that both of them chose and wanted, and they always found a way to make things work and be all right for all of us.

Chapter 6
Subtle Differences
of Operation

SOME OF THINGS THAT MY PARENTS DID differently were pretty subtle, and unless you were really looking out for them, you'd probably never even notice that they did anything different. I never really thought too much about it when I was a kid because I was just used to how my parents did things. Along the way, I realized that the way some things were done by my parents had more to do with blindness, and not just because that's how everybody else did them.

Most people wouldn't even notice that my parents got into a car a little differently than a sighted person, but I did. When you're sighted, you might just open the door and plop down into the seat. That's how I get in, anyway. If you were to really watch how a blind person does it, you might not pick up on the subtle differences. I didn't really notice until I tried to get into my car with my eyes closed, and swiftly bumped my head. Every time I tried to get into my car with my eyes closed, the same thing happened. So the next time my mom or dad got into my car, I watched. That's really when I realized my mom and dad approached that everyday task a little differently. My parents placed their hands on the top of the car at the door frame, so they knew by feel how far they need to bend down to get in. After seeing what my mom did, I tried it. And I was able to get into my car without bumping my head. Since every car is different, placing their hand on the top gives them a physical reference point for how far they need to bend down before getting in, no matter what car it is. It's the little things like this that people don't realize blind people need to accommodate so that they can do the same things as sighted people. Everyday things that children learn are just a little different with blind parents.

My parents would amaze me sometimes. When I was a small girl, out with my mom, once in a while she'd accidentally drop a coin. She would always ask me to pick up the coin: "Laura, can you find the nickel I just dropped?" Well, I was pretty young and I would always say back to her: "If it's not a nickel, can I keep it?" Always hoping it was a quarter, or at least a dime. But I was amazed that every single time, I found the coin that my mom had dropped. And every single time, it was exactly what she had asked me to find for her. I never got to keep any of the money I found, because she was always right. For years, as a little girl, I was stumped by this phenomenon. I didn't know how she knew which coins had fallen. She would always tell me whenever I asked her how she knew, "I just know what my money is." She never really gave up her "secrets."

But as I grew, I got a little wiser. I'd say to myself: "Okay, I know she can't see. So how does she know which coins she dropped?" One day at home, I closed my eyes and dropped some different coins on the floor, listening to each one as they hit the floor. And was I surprised to learn that each coin *sounded* different—because of its size, shape, and the material it was made from. I practiced and practiced until I had memorized what each coin sounded like. So there really wasn't any "secret" to my mother's accuracy with the dropped coins. She had just used her ears, when most everyone else uses their sight. When I was little, I just thought that my mom was a good guesser!

My brother and I were always amazed by the things my mom and dad seemed to know. When we were being scolded for doing something wrong, and maybe weren't really paying much attention but knew that we needed to answer back, "Yes, Mom," or, "Yes, Dad," they would commonly get angry and implore, "Look at me when I'm talking to you!" What? As a little kid, I would think, *How did they know I wasn't looking?* Sometimes I would lie and say that I *was* looking at them, because I didn't want to get in more trouble or make my parents any angrier than they were already. But they always knew.

I didn't realize as a kid that you can definitely tell the difference between someone who is talking directly to you or someone who has their head turned–because their voice sounds different. My brother and I didn't get away with very much, because our parents always seemed to know everything. It wasn't always about knowing what we were up to; they just always seemed to be able to do everyday things without much effort.

When my mom poured my brother and me a glass of milk for dinner, she'd grab the glass like anyone else, grab the milk carton and just start pouring. She'd always fill the glass close to the top, and she rarely spilled. I didn't know how she did it. She couldn't see how big the glass was, or how full it was getting as she poured. My friends, and even some adults that came over, were amazed how my mom could pour drinks into a glass without being able to see. Unless you have to rely on your other senses, you don't really think there's another way but to use your sight. But that's where hearing comes in again. As the drink is poured into the glass or cup, it makes a different sound as it gets closer and closer to the rim. So she'd pour until it sounded close to full, and then she'd stop. Later, on when she got a little older though, I also noticed that she sometimes stuck her finger into the cup while holding it and just poured until the drink reached her finger. Either way, she and my dad both managed to pour drinks into glasses without much effort—to the amazement of everyone that simply watched.

My mom was a good cook, and I loved watching her make dinner for us. She had an old Zenith radio that was about the size of a modern microwave oven, sitting on the counter. When she was cooking, it was always blaring country music. I can still see my mom cooking, wearing a dress and heels, just like all the other housewives did back then. She would wear an apron tied around her waist. A towel to wipe her hands would be slung over her shoulder, and she would be singing and smiling and swaying to the country music as she fixed our dinner. I didn't realize that when she cooked she was doing things a little differently because she was blind. She was just my mom cooking us dinner.

As I Saw It

Figure 20: Just like my mom and dad's old Zenith radio

My mom made a lot of casseroles for dinner back then, partly because they were popular. She made most of them using Campbell's mushroom soup. All the soup cans were located on the same shelf in the same cupboard in our house, but not all of them were cans of mushroom soup. There would be chicken noodle, tomato, chicken with rice, and whatever else my brother and I threw into the shopping cart at the grocery store. But my mom was always able to pick out the mushroom soup—every time. When I would watch her in the kitchen, I'd see her grab a can and shake it, put it down if it wasn't the mushroom soup, and keep picking up cans and shaking them until she found the right one. I didn't realize that cans of food shook differently and made different sounds based on what was inside. It wasn't just soup that she shook. My mom shook every single can that she took out of the cupboard.

For a long time, I thought all canned food had to be shaken before you could open the can and use it. I didn't realize that my mom was only shaking it so she could determine what was inside. After all, the labels on the cans didn't include Braille! Every once in a while, she would make a mistake and open a wrong can. Sometimes she'd have tomato soup ready as a snack when we came home from school, in part because she had mistaken the can of tomato soup for mushroom soup. Other times we'd ask her what we were having for dinner, and she'd tell us what she was making. When we sat down to eat, we'd have a different vegetable instead of the one she said. Back then, I never really knew why, and I didn't really mind. I didn't realize that she just wasn't paying very much attention when she grabbed the can and had simply opened the "wrong" vegetable. It didn't happen very often.

Some of the things in our house were adapted because our parents were blind. All the appliances, for example, were marked so that my parents could use them using touch or sound. Our oven and stove had markings on the dials. The oven would have a mark at each 100-degree increment. So if my mom needed to cook something at 350 degrees, she would turn the dial up three and a half markings. She even had a kitchen timer that had similar markings to use when she was cooking. The markings on our appliances were sometimes handmade, just glued pieces of toothpicks that someone would craft for them. It was nothing really professional. A little later on, manufacturers started marking appliances for blind people when knobs could be special ordered. I've seen our appliances marked with pieces of toothpicks, little dots of metal, and sometimes just dots of ordinary glue. Both the washer and dryer in our house were marked the same way. All my parents would have to do is memorize the increments of the markings on each appliance, which always seemed easy enough for them to do. Those weren't the usual things that led to mishaps; my parents had that stuff down.

The clock in our house chimed, so my parents always knew about what time it was. It chimed every fifteen minutes. At fifteen minutes, it would play a chord, then at the half hour it would add to it, and at forty-five minutes, more chords would be added. At the hour, it would play a whole tune and then play a chime once for each hour. All of us knew what time it was, and even my brother and I hardly ever had to look at the clock. My mom and dad also had Braille watches which they could use to tell time when they were not at home. Whenever they wanted to know the time, they would push in the button, and the glass crystal would spring open. They felt what time it was by the direction of the hands and the Braille markings for the numbers.

Everyone today uses their mobile phones to tell time, but back in those days, people wore watches to tell time—but not everyone wore them, either. It was funny, out in public, having blind parents with watches. It was easy for me to tell when some was looking to see what time it was, because they would start looking at everyone's wrist to find someone that was wearing a watch so they could ask them the time. People would look at my parents' wrist, see the watch, and start asking them for the time before they realized that they were blind. Sometimes they would just say, "Oh, sorry" and walk away before my parents could tell them.

Sometimes people would ask my parents for the time, not realizing they were blind; but they sure knew afterwards when the watch opened up and they started feeling for the time. People were very shocked to see the watches open up, most of them had never seen a Braille watch. Then, when my mom or dad felt the time, frequently the stranger was embarrassed that they had just asked a blind person for the time. Most of the time people would just say thank you, and move on. Others would walk away and keep looking back, like they just couldn't believe that a blind person had just told them the time. Sometimes when my mom or dad told someone what time it was, the person didn't trust that a blind person even knew how to tell time, so I'd see them look around for another person to ask. Too bad there were no camera phones back then to record some of these reactions. They were pretty amusing, at least to us kids.

Figure 21: Braille watch just like my dad's

Sometimes my parents used their blindness to their advantage. When we were younger and our parents didn't want us to know what they were talking about, they would just spell things to each other. Then we got older and learned how to read, and they couldn't get away with that anymore. But they had a secret weapon to use. It was Braille. After spelling things to each other didn't work, they turned to spelling things to one another using the Braille alphabet. They would say things like, "dot 1, dot 234" to spell out the words. My brother and I were stumped. They had one over us there, because we never learned how to read or write Braille. It wasn't like we needed it to learn it to communicate with our parents, like deaf children would need to learn sign language. So we just never did.

As mentioned before, my parents went to movies. They also watched television. Just because they can't see, they still use the word "watch" just like everyone else does. They don't say that they are going to go *listen* to a movie. Most people were surprised to learn that my mom and dad took us to the movies. But they liked them, too. Most of the time they could follow along pretty well. Just like if a sighted person has the TV on in another room. They're listening, but can't see the TV. Just think of it that way. You can pretty much know what's going on just by listening, but every once in a while, you have to run into the other room to watch because you want to see what's going on, or don't understand what's going on because the dialog has stopped and only background music remains. That's when my brother and I would have to tell them what was going on. It seemed that it always happened for big, pivotal scenes too. Kissing scenes, chase scenes, sometimes someone was dying, but it always seemed to be something big going on, so figuring out the rest of the movie without it was sometimes hard because something big was missed. Not all movies were like this, and my mom and dad also commonly watched TV by themselves.

My dad would always go into the other room and watch western movies. No one else liked them, so he would watch them alone.

Laura Schriner

My brother and I would read the TV guide to let them know what was going to be on for the week, so they could plan what they wanted to watch, back then there were no DVRs or other devices to record the TV shows back then. They were good at memorizing, or taking things down. Blind people can't just write Post-it notes to themselves, but they can make Braille notes. It's not as easy to make a Braille note as it is to make a written note, though. It takes a few more steps.

My parents wrote Braille two different ways. They used a Braille writer, which is similar to a typewriter, except that it has only six keys that correspond to the Braille cell locations. Alternatively, they used a slate and stylus, which is a manual way to write Braille, more similar to using a pen or pencil with a stencil. The slate is a template of individual Braille cells. The slate clamps to a piece of Braille paper to hold the paper in place and serves to line up the Braille cells across the page in a straight line. Think of it as lines drawn on a piece of paper. It's much easier to write a sentence straight on a piece of paper that has lines than it is on a blank piece of paper. The slate is a little more involved because each Braille letter has to fit into an accurately spaced Braille cell. The stylus is a short tool used to punch the different cells of the Braille cell to form letters. The stylus punches the paper, but only raises the paper slightly instead of punching actual holes.

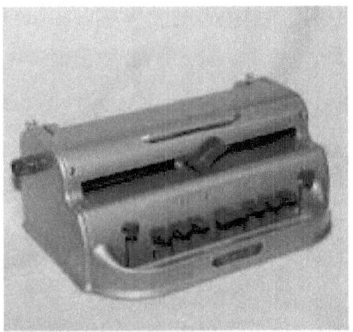

Figure 22: Braille writer

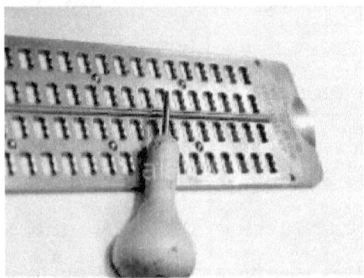

Figure 23: Slate and stylus

My mom and dad were a lot different from each other in the way they did certain things, also. My dad used a cane. It is how he learned to get around at OCB at first, and that's all he ever used. My mom, on the other hand, starting using a guide dog in 1971 to get around by herself. She had to spend the whole summer at Guide Dogs for the Blind in San Rafael, California, learning how to work with her dog and how to take care of it. My brother and I stayed at our grandparents' house that summer. When we came home, my mom had her first guide dog, and Heiress was her name. She was a beautiful, deep red Golden Retriever. She was such a deep red color that she looked like an Irish Setter. She was mom's working dog when my mom needed her, but when she was home, she was our family pet, too. My brother and I would play with her for hours. She would play hide and seek with us. My brother and I would hide and my mom would say, "Heiress, go find them." Heiress would sniff around and find us hiding in the closet or underneath the bed.

My brother and I thought it was the greatest thing that our dog could come with us into restaurants, grocery stores, doctors' offices, and anyplace else. If any place ever questioned my mom bringing in her guide dog, she would show them her card, which stated the law for guide dogs. Heiress would be fed once a day at the same time. My mom would take her outside to go potty at the same time every day as well. That way we knew when Heiress had to go to the bathroom when she was working. My mom knew that if it was getting close to Heiress's potty time, she'd have to stop what she was doing and find a place for her to go. Heiress was on a strict schedule in part so that she could go out in public and go into stores or restaurants with my mom, and my mom could take care of business without worrying that Heiress might have a potty accident in the store.

Figure 24: My mom and Heiress the guide dog, taken in 1971

Some of the difference in my parents' respective approaches to tasks was probably due to the fact that my mom was born blind and my dad went blind later in his life. My mom seemed much more at ease being blind than my dad ever did. She was graceful. She could walk around our house and not bump into anything, she seemed to always know where other things were in relation to her movements. My dad, on the other hand, seemed to always be bumping into things. He'd would gently take his hand and touch the wall, using it as a guide when he walked down the hallway, but every time he did that, he knocked some pictures off the wall. So if we wanted decorations or pictures on the wall, they would have to be hung really high. He'd walk by tables and bump into them and things would fall to the floor. It wouldn't happen all the time, just enough to make us be very careful where we put things, especially things that were easily broken. If we happened to set something on a table, it just might be broken and on the floor when we saw it next. So we learned to put our stuff away, or sometimes lose it.

Our pets learned about our dad too. When Heiress was lying on the floor sound asleep, she would wake up and move to a new place simply because she heard my dad coming close to her. If she didn't get up and move, he usually stepped on her, and she figured that out pretty early. When my mom was walking around and Heiress was sleeping on the floor, Heiress would just lay there, sleeping away. My mom would brush by Heiress perhaps, barely waking her up. Same with our cats; if any of our cats were sleeping on the sofa or in a chair and they heard my dad coming, they'd jump out. They knew that my dad usually wouldn't check to see if they were resting there before he sat down. And they'd been sat on many times before! Our pets had to learn the hard way, but they were smart enough to get out of his way. My brother and I also had to worry about getting stepped on by our dad too. Sometimes we'd be watching TV on the floor, but instead of getting up and running away, we'd just tell him where we were and he'd manage to walk around us.

Other people were just astonished by the ease with which my parents got around and were able to accomplish everyday things. It wasn't that my parents were doing anything special, but many people in that era just hadn't realized how capable and how independent blind people can really be with just a little support and training. I was constantly hearing people tell my parents, "Wow, you can do that better than me." What sighted people don't realize is that blind people are doing things with a little different twist, using a different way of sensing things. Just like I didn't realize that my parents were doing things any special way until I investigated some of the things I couldn't do with my eyes closed. Many others watching don't even pick up on the fact a blind person is even making subtle accommodations in lieu of sight.

Chapter 7
Being Me, Seeing Things Differently

I WAS AWARE THAT MY PARENTS WERE blind from a very young age. I was actually intrigued by their blindness and wondered how they could do some of the things they did without seeing. But I always felt the need to watch over them, too, so people didn't take advantage of them. I wanted to protect them. My brother didn't feel the same way that I did, and he never really had the same wonder about their blindness that I did. The other kids I knew who had blind parents didn't feel the same way as me either, so I'm not sure where this feeling that I needed to protect them and my curiosity for their blindness came from. I guess it stemmed from just realizing they were different, and having more empathy. I could see it, of course, and so could most everyone else. I think it was being the eldest child that made me feel the obligation, like it was my job or my duty to watch out for them.

Blindness always seemed to be on my mind when I was young. When I started playing house, I would pretend to be a blind mommy, not a sighted one. I would close my eyes and hold my dolls. I would try to dress them with my eyes shut. I would even push them around in their stroller with my eyes shut until I bumped into something, or got hurt pretending to be blind. I wanted to pretend to be a mommy just like my own mom.

I also walked around the house sometimes with my eyes closed, just to see if I could do it like my parents did. It wasn't easy, though. I'd always bump into things, and I can tell you that the coffee table hurts when you run into it and bump your shins. It also hurts when misjudging a turn and you walk hard into the corner of the wall. One time when I had my eyes closed, my hands just happened to be spread out far enough that one hand went to one side of the wall and the other hand to the other side. I thought I had just walked into the next room, but then, bam, I ran right into the corner, face first. Hitting the corner of that wall was the last time I ever walked in our house with my eyes closed pretending to be blind.

I still tried it outdoors, though. I'd play a guessing game with myself. As I walked to our house from the corner of the street, I'd close my eyes for a while and before I opened them, I'd try to guess whose house I was standing in front of, simply by counting the driveways that I was walking past. I'm not sure why I did this, other than just being bored, because I would only do it when my friends weren't around.

One day, I got the hare-brained idea that I would try to ride my bike pretending that I was blind, but that didn't turn out well at all. I started riding in the middle of the road at the bottom of our street. Every few seconds, I would try to guess how far I'd travelled, then open my eyes to see if I was right. I did this a few times, but hadn't really made it very far up the street before I hit a brand new car parked on the side of the street. It was so new it didn't even have license plates yet. The grips on my handlebars were long gone, so when I hit the side of the car, the metal of my handlebar scraped the paint—all the way down. I remember opening my eyes and seeing the big scratch. I was terrified... and embarrassed. "Who tries to ride a bike with their eyes shut? What a dumb idea," I thought.

I was just getting ready to sneak off, when I heard a voice from the porch, "Are you okay?" *Yikes, they saw me,* I thought to myself. When you do something that stupid, you don't want anyone to know about it. But I was busted! I felt the terror inside, and managed to say a faint "Yes" with a shaky, embarrassed voice. Then they asked me, "Is the car okay?" I was so terrified at what I had done that I lied and said, "Yes!" I jumped on my bike and rode as fast as I could back to my house and ran into my room and shut the door. I sat there and hoped they wouldn't see the scratch, that this would all just go away. But a few minutes later, the dreaded knock on the door came.

Please, please, please mom, don't hear the knock, don't answer the door, I thought to myself, but she did. And, yes, it was the neighbors, the ones whose car I had just scratched. They told my mom that I ran into their car with my bicycle, but what they didn't know was that I had my eyes closed pretending to be blind when I did it. My mom called my name with that authoritative voice that I always hated: "Laura, come out here." She asked me, "Did you do that?" I lied and told her that I didn't see a scratch, so that's why I left and rode home. The neighbors said they would take it into the dealership and let my mom know how much. It turns out that the dealer suggested only a touch-up paint job, and the cost was only

$20. I was still in big trouble, but my mom wasn't as mad when it turned out to be only $20. Thank goodness our neighbors were such nice people, because it could have turned out much worse.

My parents never knew that I pretended to be blind. In fact, I've never told anyone until this writing. I was definitely embarrassed to say anything when I'd get hurt, or when I'd done something stupid like running into the car. And think to myself, *I'm not blind. I can see. Why did I do that?* I chastised myself like that every single time. But I guess that I was just a curious kid and wanted to know what it felt like to be blind.

I always felt like I had to protect my parents, mainly because I didn't want them to get cheated because they are blind. So I was always on the lookout to make sure it didn't happen when I was around. But sometimes that protectiveness I felt got out of hand, and went farther than just keeping my parents safe from being cheated out of money, and I would end up making some adults pretty angry. That's why I think I asked so many questions—so I'd always be aware of what was going on.

I was in the car with my grandpa Woody once, when I was five or six years old. I was curious about driving, since my parents didn't drive, of course. On this particular trip, I started asking him lots and lots of questions. I asked him what the speedometer was and what it meant. He told me it showed how fast the car was going, and then he showed me how to read it. He pointed out the speed limit signs on the side of the road, and told me that the numbers on the signs were how fast he was allowed to drive. He said that if he drove any faster than what the sign showed, he could get in trouble by the police for breaking the law, be pulled over, and get a ticket.

So I took what I learned from my grandpa, and started to look at the speedometer in all the taxis when we were riding in them. I'd look for the speed limit signs to see how fast we were supposed to go, and then look to see how fast the taxi driver was going. If he was going too fast, I'd tell on him. "Mamma, the man is going too fast. He is breaking the law." I don't think that my mom and dad really knew what to do with me when I said things like that out loud in front of strangers, and I probably surprised the heck out of them with the things that I'd learned. They would always just tell me that it was okay. But sometimes I would insist that it wasn't okay to break the law. Most of the times, the taxi drivers would slow down, and I'd make sure they slowed down to the correct speed. Other times they would get upset that the little girl in the back seat was telling them they were doing something wrong.

I would also make sure the taxi drivers weren't charging us too much money. I knew all the streets and routes where we lived very well, from taking buses all the time. I would tell my mom that the cab driver doesn't know where he is going, he is taking us the long way, and was going to charge us too much. Most of the time it wasn't exactly true, because they were just taking us the best way they knew, but once in while it was exactly what was happening. They'd be taking the long way to get more money. Usually, the taxi driver would be embarrassed that a little girl had just ratted him out, and some of those taxi drivers would charge us less than what the meter showed when we got home.

Each taxi driver had a different response to me, but most of them were pretty nice about it. One taxi driver didn't like it at all. He told my mom that if I didn't shut up, he was going to kick us out of the cab because he had enough. So my mom hushed me the rest of the ride home. One driver actually told my mom, "I feel like my mother-in-law is in the car. No, she's even worse than a mother-in-law!" I'm not sure how I became such a brave little girl, standing up to adults like that, but I always kept everyone on their toes. It didn't end with taxi drivers when I spoke my mind. I did it when we were out clothes shopping, too.

When I was just three or four years old, I started telling my mom things like, "Mama, that dress is ugly. Don't buy it. This one is prettier." "Oooh, Mama, you look pretty in that dress." And sometimes my opinion wasn't very nice: "Mama, she's lying, because that dress is ugly," when the lady helping us at the department store was telling my mom something I didn't agree with. My mom started listening to what I had to say, and started buying the dresses that I thought were pretty—not the recommendations from the lady at the store helping us. My mom always got compliments on the dresses I picked out, too. People would ask her, "Who picked out your dress, Diane?"

"My daughter did," she would tell them proudly. They would look down at me in disbelief. I mean, I was just three or four years old and still playing in the racks of clothes at the time. I would just look up at these people and smile as they stared back in disbelief. Those were proud moments for me as a little girl!

That's pretty much how I started doing most other things for my parents that usually only adults did, and that's how I ended up with the chores that I did. My chores were definitely different than what my friends had to do around their houses. I didn't have to sweep the garage, or take out the trash, feed the pets, or any of the other things that all my friends had to do. And I loved not having those chores! My chores were instead comprised of all the grownup stuff that my parents couldn't do themselves. I'd start telling my parents things that I thought I could do, or asking if they would let me do something. If they had a need, I'd usually at least get to try.

When I was nine years old, I heard my mom and dad complaining that the bills had been returned in the mail because the person who was helping them didn't do it right. So the next time the lady showed up to make out the money orders to pay the bills, I sat down at the table with her and watched how she did it. When some of the bills came back again the second month in a row, and I saw that my mom and dad were very frustrated, I told them that I knew how to do it. My mom and dad were hesitant to let me try, but I convinced them that I could.

The first month I did it, my mom ran out to the mail every day afterwards looking to find a bill that had been returned. But nothing showed up, and she didn't get any calls that she was late. So she let me do it again the next month. Again, no problems. So I *did* know how to do it. And that's how I ended up paying the bills every month. It didn't stop with just paying the bills; I started to fill out all the forms and completing all forms of paperwork that came in the mail too, and this lasted pretty much the rest of my life until I moved out of the house. I really didn't mind doing these things, unless my friends were outside playing and I was stuck inside.

One thing that I wasn't too fond of was being out in public as a family where we really stood out. It was an unusual sight to see two blind parents being led by two small children, and because of this, people always gawked at us. It happened when my brother and I were with just one of our parents, too. I was really bothered by it, so I started to call out the people who stared. We couldn't go anywhere without people staring. People would sometimes walk into each other or bump into poles or buildings because they were so entranced watching us. Whenever I caught someone staring, most people would usually just turn their head away and stop staring. But some of the gawkers didn't. I guess they didn't care if a little kid saw that they were staring, because even when I would turn around and catch them looking at us, they would just keep staring. I knew it was rude to stare, and that's probably why I didn't like them to do it, but they kept on doing it. One day, I just got so frustrated that I started to stand up for me and my parents. I was about four years old at the time. There was this woman who would not take her eyes off of us, so I spoke up and asked her, "What are you looking at?"

My mother would get embarrassed every time I did that and would just tell me, "It's okay, honey; they're just curious." But my parents couldn't see to realize how uncomfortable and creepy it was to look up and realize that someone, an adult, had been staring at you for a long time, and they were still staring.

As I child, I did not comprehend what all the curiosity was about. But people continued to gawk at us. As I got older, instead of saying something, I would sometimes just stare back. Other times, I'd rest my head on my hands and really stare them down. They got the hint then. The gawkers would get embarrassed when they realized what I was doing, and I would think that maybe I just prevented this person from staring the next time they saw us. Those were proud moments when I realized that I could turn the tables and give them a taste of their own medicine. This way, just staring back, my mom or dad wouldn't be the wiser, and it empowered me knowing that the offenders got the point.

Going grocery shopping didn't seem as bad to me, because I was mostly focused on getting what we needed instead of making sure people weren't staring. My brother had a different opinion, though. Grocery shopping didn't make his list of favorite things. I actually thought grocery shopping was a treat and looked forward to doing it, because then I'd get to pick out all the things that I liked to eat. I hated when I wasn't home and my brother went instead, because he'd pick out what he liked and would always forget something that I really wanted. My mother always liked it better when I went, too. I thought she liked going with me because I was a better shopper, but that wasn't the case at all.

I don't think my brother minded going grocery shopping with my mom when he was younger. I think he started to dread going when he was in high school. It wasn't that he dreaded grocery shopping itself, but he dreaded the thought of running into someone he knew from school. I wasn't nearly as concerned about it as my brother was. Yeah, I didn't really want to run into anyone that might know me from school, but if that happened, I would just push the grocery cart down a different aisle or pretend that I didn't see them.

My brother, I found out, had a whole different way of handling the situation. When we were grocery shopping with our mom, she would hold onto the grocery cart while my brother or I pushed it and steered it around the store. One time, my brother and I both took my mom grocery shopping at the same time. It was a pretty rare occasion that both of us went. I was pushing the grocery cart with my mom holding on, and then we thought of something we needed from a different aisle that we had forgotten. So my brother took over pushing the cart, and I went to get the item that we had missed.

When I was searching the store to find my mom and brother, I was shocked to see my mom standing in the middle of the aisle, holding onto the grocery cart by herself. I asked her, "Where's David?" She replied, "He saw someone he knew and took off." I thought she meant was that he was off goofing around with a friend from school, but that's not what she meant exactly. He just walked away from her and left her standing, maybe so the person from school wouldn't know that he had blind parents. My mom and I shopped for another whole 15 or 20 minutes before he returned. And that's what he'd do every time he was out with my mom alone, if he happened to see someone he knew from school. I couldn't believe that my brother just left my mom standing alone and helpless like that. But he did. I guess I knew why my mom liked shopping with me better. It wasn't because I was a better shopper; it was because she just didn't like being abandoned.

Shopping for toys was the best part of our shopping experiences when we were kids. My mom and dad would sometimes take us to the toy store and let us pick out what we wanted. But sometimes picking out something on our own made for a challenge to be had after we got home, especially when we were so young we didn't know how to read yet. Sometimes we'd not have realized that our toy needed batteries, so we'd have to wait until the next time we went out before we could play with it. Sometimes what we picked out needed to be assembled, and by an adult's capable hand. That wasn't too much fun either, because sometimes my brother and I couldn't figure out how to put it together. So we'd have to wait for a neighbor to help us, or we'd try it ourselves and end up breaking a piece. At times, we'd pick out toys that were way beyond our years.

So my mom and dad got a little wiser as time went on. When we were really little, she would make sure to ask the clerk all the questions about what we had picked out. Does it need batteries? Does it need to be put together? Is this toy age-appropriate? Based on the clerk's feedback, they wouldn't let us buy it unless they knew for sure that we were going to get home and then be disappointed by something we had overlooked. As we got older, our parents started asking us the same questions. If we didn't know or couldn't answer them, asking the clerk was the next step. If we didn't know how to use it or how to put it together after talking to the clerk, we couldn't buy it. There were lots of times we didn't get what we wanted as a result. But most of the time everything worked out, and my brother and I were happy little kids playing with our new toys.

Having blind parents sometimes gave my friends a different perspective on things, too. Since we didn't have a car and my parents couldn't drive, any time our friends came with us they'd have to ride in a taxi or take the buses with us. I was envious of my friends, because they and their families could just get in the car and drive whenever they wanted, while we always had to schedule things to make sure a taxi or bus was available or working at the time we needed. To my friends, it was no big deal to have a car. And to me, it was no big deal to ride in a taxi or on a bus. But when my friends would come along with us and ride in a taxi, it was an experience like no other for them. They would end up talking about it for days. My friends even thought that my family was rich, because their parents had told them that only rich people take taxis.

Having blind parents influenced my life quite a bit, and even my friends' lives at times. When I was growing up, I never really thought that my experiences were different from any other person just because my parents were blind. It all seemed quite normal to me. We did what we needed to do to get by, and got help from friends and other people if we needed it.

My friends with blind parents didn't all have the same experiences that I had. Their parents didn't rely on them as heavily as my mom and dad relied on me. Just like with any relationship, whether with sighted or blind people, when people start doing things for you, you start to rely on them more and more. It wasn't really intentional that my blind parents needed my help or that they anticipated relying so much on their sighted daughter. They did most everything themselves before I came along. It was true that I wanted to help and make their lives easier—so they became used to my help the same way you might hire someone to clean your house. You know you can do it on your own when you have to, but it is so much nicer when you have someone else who can do it for you.

Chapter 8
School Days, Kids and Dad Alike

I DON'T THINK MY SCHOOL EXPERIENCE WAS much different for me because my parents were blind, but my perception of the differences between me and our family and the other kids was definitely heightened once I went to school. My parents couldn't see what I looked like when they sent me off to school. There were plenty of times that I'm sure my teachers' eyes bugged out by the way I looked, but that's because my parents couldn't see odd things when I walked out the door. I'd go to school sometimes with bright red Kool-Aid mustaches, stains on my clothes that hadn't come out in the wash, or hair that wasn't brushed or tied back very well. These were the kinds of things my parents couldn't really feel were wrong, and I was definitely too young to notice or care myself. Most of the time it was just little things, but most sighted parents just wouldn't let their children out of the house that way.

School projects weren't fun to tackle, having blind parents. The projects could take weeks of planning and putting together. Most kids get their parents to help out with those, and well, my parents couldn't really help me. I would work for weeks getting my project planned and put together. I'd struggle and cry sometimes when it wouldn't go together easily. My mom would always ask me if she could help, but she really couldn't. So I struggled and made my projects the best that I could on my own. I was proud of what I'd done—until I got to school. I'd have to put my imperfect and rigged-together project next to all the flawless looking ones my friends brought. Yeah, I knew that their parents helped them, and that's why they looked so good, but that still didn't make me feel very positive about mine. That proud feeling that I'd had while carrying it to school quickly turned into utter embarrassment when I saw the other projects. Even more embarrassing was when the other kids at school asked, "Which one is yours?" My stomach just sank. I just wanted to run home and hide.

The teachers knew that my parents were blind, and that as a result, I did mine purely on my own. So they would always take that into consideration when evaluating, even though I didn't really realize it. When grades were given, I'd always get very good grades. Then I would ask the other kids what grades they got. I was shocked that my grade was better than theirs, because their projects looked so much better than mine. When I found out the other kids' grades, I was embarrassed by my grade. I always felt that my teacher felt sorry for me, and just gave me a good grade because my parents were blind. It wasn't until I got older that I realized that I got better grades because I genuinely had done all the work myself.

Even though my mom wasn't able to help me with putting together my projects, she was able to help with some of my homework for a while. She helped me learn my times tables, and solve addition and subtraction problems when I read them to her. The rest of the time, I did my homework by myself. Every once in a while, I would have to ask a neighbor how to do something, because my mom didn't know what the heck I was asking her. When I was in high school, history was my worst subject. I'd have to read long chapters, sometimes several of them at a time, and then answer questions afterwards.

I hated reading, and my comprehension didn't seem very good, because I couldn't just read a chapter and remember enough to answer the questions at the end. I'd have to go back and re-read entire sections all the time. Sometimes when I re-read parts of the book, I still couldn't answer the questions. That's when my mom's great memory came in handy. She was really good at history homework. She was very patient with me, too. She would sit by me and listen while I read the chapter out loud. Afterwards, she helped answer all the questions, or was at least able to point me to the sections that contained the answer. I would not have been able to pass history class without my mom's help.

My mom also helped my brother with his schoolwork at home, and sometimes creatively. My brother was born near-sighted and had to wear glasses from the time he was 18 months old. He started to develop a lazy eye and some other visual problems as a result of his nearsightedness. He had to have multiple surgeries during the same school year once. Because of all the school he missed, he fell way behind the other students, and had to be held back a year when he was in second grade.

When he went back to school, he couldn't keep up with the other kids in reading. So my mom ordered the same set of books, in Braille versions, as he was reading in his class. Every single night, my brother would sit down alongside my mother with his printed book, while she followed along with her Braille book, so she could help him when he struggled with words. Alternatively, she would read to him from her book until he learned all the words. My brother was able to catch up in his reading, and there were never any issues after that.

One thing my mom and dad never did was come to any school performances. There was always a school performance at the end of the year, during which each grade would have to perform either a song or a skit. It would be in the evening, and all the parents would come, but not mine. I think that my mom came to the very first one, but it was a pretty awkward experience for her. I would have to take her over there really early, at the same time as I had to be there for final preparations. She'd just sit in a chair in the audience, all by herself, while all the kids got ready. When all the other parents started coming in to the audience, they would ignore her. She just sat in the same chair while all the kids performed. No one talked to her or said anything. She'd be sitting in that same chair for hours and hours until I was able to come back to get her, and by then most everyone had already gone home. She couldn't even use the restroom during that time, because there was no one to show her were it was. So after that, she never did come to anything else. I really can't blame her. My mom did a lot for us and went out of her way for some things, but school performances were a step too far.

Parents' night at the school was something else that could become quite awkward. Parents' night was for the parents, yet I had to be there to guide my mom to my class. The teacher was busy with all the different parents on that night, so she really couldn't take my mom's arm and show her all the different projects the teacher had put up around the room for this evening. So I had to stay with my mom, walking her to the different projects that were up, and tell her about them. Every so often, the teacher would come back and talk to us.

Most awkward was that this was the night that the teacher was also supposed to tell the parents how their children were doing in class. Sometimes teachers would just tell my mom with me there, but every once in a while, the teacher would tell me to go look at something on the other side of the room for a minute if she needed to tell my mom anything that I wasn't supposed to hear. The first time I took my mom, I sat her in the classroom and thought the teacher would stop by, but I was wrong. My mom just sat there alone. So that's why I stayed with her. Some of the teachers knew what to do, but some of them were just as awkward as anyone else about knowing what to do to facilitate, or even how to behave when a blind person was around.

There were perks having blind parents. Most every year in elementary school, each grade got to go on a field trip. One year, I got to go on two different field trips. I was in fifth grade and went with my class. But I also got to go on the fourth graders' field trip too. My fifth grade teacher announced in class that the fourth graders were going to Sutter's Fort in Sacramento, and that there were two extra seats on the bus. She said there were going to be two lucky fifth graders that were going to be able to go to Sutter's Fort with the fourth grade. Well, one of them just happened to be me. They said they drew names from a hat, but I think they were lying. The other person that got to go on that extra trip was the poorest kid in my class. So it seemed that all three of the fifth grade teachers chose based on who might never get to go to those places on their own. It seemed apparent to me, but I don't think the other kids noticed what happened. I felt lucky to go in any event.

When we were absent or needed to get out of school early, I'd write my own note and then my mom or dad would sign it. When absent the day before, I'd have to go to the office and get a slip so that I could get back into class, just like all the other students. The first time I went to the office with my note it caused a big stir. The secretary in the office told me, "Well, you wrote this note." So I had to tell her, "Yes, my parents are blind. I wrote it and then they signed it." The first time this happened, the secretary had to go ask someone if my note was okay before she gave me my slip of paper to get back to class. It was really embarrassing, because all the students who were absent the day before were all lined up behind me, waiting and listening. They would hear everything that I was saying, and then have to wait for the secretary to get back to get their own slips. It was embarrassing that all the other kids could hear me and knew my business, and that the adults had trouble believing me, too.

One time, my mom told me to just sign for her. So I did. The secretary at the office didn't say anything or question my signature. So that's what I did from then on. Everyone in the office knew what was going on, so it was really no big deal. Well, in grade school, at least. Then, when I went to middle school, I'd have to go through the same process of verification each time I went to a new school. They would question me. I'd tell them that my parents were blind. Maybe they'd check out my story. Then the rest of the year would be okay.

One day I had a doctor's appointment, and as a result I had to leave school a little early. I told my teacher that I needed to leave, like I had always done in the past with my other teachers. Usually, the teacher just asked if I had a note, and then would send me to the office to sign out for the day so I could leave campus. But this time, my teacher wanted me to show her the note. So I showed it to her. Well, it was in my handwriting, and of course she knew my handwriting. So she took me outside and questioned me. I told her that my parents were blind and that I had been signing my parents name for a long time. She thought I was lying just to get out of her class. She interrogated me for a few minutes, and then she called my counselor and told him that she thought I was lying just to get out of her English class. It was almost like she took it as a personal affront, and she was outraged.

I had to go down to my counselor's office. When I walked into his office, he shut the door behind me. Usually when the door was shut, that meant someone was getting in trouble. He accused me of lying and writing my own note—not because I had a doctor's appointment, but because I just wanted to get out of class. I couldn't believe what was happening. He threatened to call my parents and tell them. In turn, I kept asking him to please call my parents and they would confirm that I had a doctor's appointment. Instead, to my horror, he insisted on interrogating me until I confessed that I really didn't have a doctor's appointment. It was one of my worst classes, with one of the worst teachers, too, so no wonder they might have been suspicious that I was just trying to leave her class. I sat in his office begging him to call either the doctor's office or my mom.

A full hour after I came to his office, he said he would call my mom. Finally! "Mrs. Phelps, I have your daughter in my office," he started the conversation. I could hear my mom's voice change when he said that. She thought that I had done something really bad, and was in a lot of trouble or something. I could tell in her voice. He continued, "She wrote her own note trying to get out of class. She said that she had a doctor's appointment and needed to leave school early." My mom said, "Yeah, so what's the problem?" "Well, she wrote her own note and signed your name," he said to my mom. My mom responded, "Well, I'm blind and it is much easier for her to write the notes than it is for me. It's how we've been doing it for a few years now." Well, my counselor didn't like that. He told my mom that was forgery, and that I couldn't do it anymore.

For the first time in my life, my mom actually stood up to my counselor. She normally would not want to make things difficult and would just go along with whatever she needed to get through without breaking rules. But this time, she told him off for not believing me, and told him that the next time I had a doctor's appointment, she would simply keep me home from school the whole day if it was going to be this hard and cause this much trouble every single time. Well, that's not what he wanted to hear either, because public schools get their money based on the number of students in the school and their attendance. So this time, the school backed down instead of my mom. The next day, I went into my English class as usual, and wanted to stick my tongue out at the teacher for all the trouble she caused. But I didn't. I felt vindicated, though. But my teacher just glared at me. I could tell that she still didn't like the fact that I wrote my own notes.

Although some situations came up in school that probably wouldn't happen in a sighted family, mostly they were no big deal. If I felt embarrassed, it was only because I saw differences between me and the other kids, and that was awkward, but that embarrassment never lasted very long. My mom and dad supported both my brother and me the best they could, and like always, everything just worked out for all of us.

• • • • • •

My dad went to school for a lot of the years my brother and I were growing up. When we lived in Hayward, the university was only a few blocks away, and he could take the city buses that were close. When we moved to Vacaville in 1971, the year my mom got her first guide dog, my dad started going to California State University at Sacramento so he could get his Master's degree in Rehabilitation Counseling. But Sacramento State was approximately 40 miles away from where we lived. When he first started going, he had to take Greyhound buses to Sacramento. The buses would stop at each town along the way. When he got to Sacramento, he had to catch city buses that stopped many times before finally arriving at the campus or else take an expensive taxi. Getting to the campus taking public transportation made for very, very long days for my dad. Each way took longer than two hours. He'd have to leave early in the morning and then wouldn't get back home until later in the evening.

After a couple of weeks, he would meet someone that was commuting from close to where we lived, and he would ride with them. My dad would pay the person's gas for the ride, and it was much cheaper and took a lot less time than catching buses. As each semester changed and schedules changed, my dad would usually have to find another person to ride with whose schedule more closely matched his own. Sometimes the people he got rides from were unreliable, and they wouldn't show up. My dad missed one of his exams one time, and he had to beg the professor to be able to take it another day. Eventually, it was too hard on my dad getting to campus every day, so my mom and dad made the decision that it would be easier for him to stay in the dorms and come home on weekends.

What was exciting about my dad going to college was that my dad was hanging around people that were only about 10 years older than me, which made him interested in the same music that I listened to at the time. When he told me his favorite song was "Freebird," by Lynyrd Skynyrd, I was shocked that I liked the same song. That Christmas, I got one of the best presents ever. My first stereo system. My dad picked out a Marantz receiver, a turntable, and huge speakers. It was all the popular and latest equipment at the time. It was all because my dad lived in the dorms. He asked one of the students he was friends with to pick it out for me. And he also bought me a couple of albums, and one of the albums of course was by Lynyrd Skynyrd. It was the best gift ever, and they hid it up in the attic that year.

The early 1970s was an important time for the feminist movement. My dad always wanted me to be a strong woman, so he would buy me books by feminist authors, and bring them home for me to read. He didn't want me relying on a man, like most of the women did from his generation. He wanted me to become a free thinker and have my own career. It was kind of funny that he wanted his daughter to be independent, but yet he wanted my mom to be the housewife from the 60s. He was the cool dad during that time.

I know that my dad had a great time living in the dorms, too, because he would always come home and tell me stories of all the fun he was having and the pranks that were going on. My dad told me that one time some of the students took a car apart, and reassembled it in a dorm room, while the guy was gone for the weekend. The students would also play pranks on my dad. They would move furniture out in the hallway so my dad would have a hard time getting to the bathroom or shower. My dad said that sometimes, he'd walk back from the shower totally nude to prank them back. He'd just walk like no one was around. Streaking, the act of running or walking around naked in public as a prank, was a big thing back then. Everyone was doing it. No one ever said anything to him, and he never got into trouble.

The students also used my dad to prank others too. They put my dad into the driver's seat of one of their cars. There was a sighted student in the car actually steering and telling my dad when to use the gas and brake pedals, but the student was crouched down so far that he couldn't be seen by onlookers. It appeared as if my dad was driving car by himself. They drove all around campus with the window down. My dad shouted and waved to all the students and professors as he drove by with his dark glasses on. He had a lot of fun in the dorms.

But school wasn't always fun and games; it was also a lot of really hard work to get his degree and that was even harder because he was blind. He had to tape record his classes instead of taking notes. My dad had to use reel-to-reel tapes for it all and carried a heavy tape recorder and several tapes around with him all the time. When he studied, he'd have to play the tapes back and listen to the whole class, instead of simply flipping pages to find the answers that he needed. It took a lot of extra time. He studied until the wee hours of the night, fast-forwarding and rewinding the reel-to-reel tapes so he didn't miss a thing. My dad also had to hire readers who would read his textbooks onto tape. So when my dad had to study for exams, he had to listen to all the tapes from his textbooks and from his lectures.

He had a full library of tapes for each class. He had to label them in Braille with the dates, the class, and a summary of what was covered in the class, so that he could find the content he needed for each exam. His dorm room was full of tapes that he kept. When finals came around, he'd have a whole library of tapes he had to listen to. He even had math classes taped. To this day, I do not know how my dad took the math classes that he did and passed them, because math is hard even for sighted people who can follow along visually. He had me read some of equations to him so that he could memorize them, and I didn't even know what I was reading to him. I'd explain the symbols to him, but I didn't even know what they were called. But he memorized all of the equations, symbols, and math signs in his head before he took his exams.

My dad made the Honors List and eventually graduated summa cum laude. I didn't know what that meant at the time, but knew it was exciting news when my father told us. He was so proud and excited to finally be done with school. It was a long, hard journey, finishing school after just going blind, yet he was determined not to let his blindness limit him. My dad never let anything get in the way of what he wanted to do and neither did my mom. When they made up their minds that they wanted to do something, they always came up with a way to accomplish it.

Chapter 9
The Things I Got Away With... or Not

MOST PEOPLE THINK THAT SINCE MY PARENTS are blind, I probably got away with a lot. Well, not as much as you might think. Believe me when I say that I tried. My brother really didn't try to get away with very much. My brother and I were definitely different people and seemed to be cut from different cloths. I guess I got some of the hoodlum from my dad's side, and my brother got some of the goody-two-shoes from my mom's side. There was a reason some of my relatives nicknamed me Little Roy. We definitely caused my parents different degrees of stress. I seemed to cause a lot more problems than my brother did, in part because I spent most of my life trying to figure what I could do and how I could get away with it. My brother, on the other hand, was a more go-with-the-flow, obedient type of kid. I used every opportunity I could to get away with things or deflect the blame. The fact that my brother was four whole years younger than me just meant that I was four years wiser, and I used every opportunity I could to my advantage.

My exploits started very, very young. I was still eating in a high chair when I first realized that I could get away with *not* eating the things I didn't like. Some kids just refuse, but I used to trick my mom into thinking that I ate everything. My mom would put the food on my tray, and if I didn't want to eat it, I would hide it in my water cup. My mom would feel the high chair and sometimes feel around the floor to make sure I hadn't dropped everything on the floor, and that way she could gauge how much I'd eaten. She didn't check my water cup until a lot later, when I was already out of the high chair. That only worked a few times on my mother, but I got away with hiding my food more often when my dad fed me, and even when my sighted grandpa Woody fed me, too.

I'm not sure why I did some of the things that I did, or how I even thought to do them in the first place. I was just a toddler when I tried to trick my mom into thinking that she didn't vacuum very well. She was very meticulous when she vacuumed. She would go over the floors several times just to make sure that she didn't miss anything, not even a speck of dust. She would move the furniture around and vacuum behind it. The laundry detergent that my mom used to wash our clothes came in tablets. Salvo laundry detergent tablets, they were called. They were easy to use because there was no measuring involved. My mom just had to toss one of the tablets into the washing machine, and that was that. Well, I got this crazy idea to break up the laundry detergent tablets behind the chair, just as my mom got done vacuuming behind it, in fact as she was moving the chair back. She didn't notice right away. So I got away with it for a couple of days. Then she thought that she might have dropped the laundry detergent. She was a little baffled how laundry detergent got behind the chair. The second time it happened, though, she knew that I was the one who made the mess.

I even tried to do things to my brother. David was on allergy and asthma medicine when he was just a couple of years old. My mom used to drop the pill he had to take into a cup of juice, and leave the cup on the kitchen counter until the pill dissolved. She would then give my brother his glass of juice to drink every night before he went to bed. When I was around six years old, I climbed up on the counter and poured some dish soap into the cup while the pill was still dissolving. I don't know what I was thinking; in my mind maybe I just wanted to see my brother blow bubbles like the cartoon characters did on TV.

When it was time to go to bed, my mom went into the kitchen and called my brother to come drink his juice. Of course, I went into the kitchen, too, so that I could see the whole thing as it unfolded. My mom reached for the cup, and just as she was about to hand it to my brother to drink, she pulled it back and smelled the cup. I guess that I put too much dish soap in it, for her to be able to smell it from an arm's reach. So my brother never drank the dish soap. Thank goodness, really! But I sure did make my parents mad. I denied doing it, but I was the only one in the house who could have. I really got in trouble and I got spanked with the belt. So I never got to see my little brother blow bubbles!

Sometimes I just wasn't very nice to my little brother. Whenever we got some candy, I'd eat all of mine pretty quickly. My brother didn't do that, he always wanted to save his. Well, that always benefitted me too, because I knew where he kept it. After all my candy was gone, I'd sneak and get his. I wouldn't take all of it, though. That would be too obvious. So I'd leave a piece or two. When he went to get some of his candy a few days later, I had already taken all of it but a couple of pieces. He would try to get me in trouble by telling our mom. But when she asked, "Did you eat your brother's candy?" I'd always reply, "No, Mom, he must have eaten it and forgot. I saw him eating some of his candy yesterday." My brother was too young to really get back at me, so I was able to get away with little things like that back then.

If I wasn't taking my brother's candy, I was trying to blame things on him that I had done. After we moved to our house in Vacaville, we were allowed to have pets. We had our mother's guide dog, but we also had a couple of cats. One was a pure white cat named Frosty, and the other was a pure gray cat named Gray. Frosty jumped onto my lap one day while I was coloring with some new markers my parents bought me. I decided that instead of coloring in my coloring book, I would color on Frosty. And I did it while my mom was sitting in the same room. I used every color I had on little Frosty, coloring his whole body and the top of his head. My parents couldn't see it, and I made sure my brother didn't say anything to my mom or dad. So I thought I could get away with it, and I did, for about a week or so. Then my mom's helper, Debbi, came over. She noticed right away, and asked my mom, "Who colored the cat?"

Of course my mom didn't know anything about it. When she asked me if I had colored the cat, I said "Mom, do you think I would do something that stupid?" It worked! That one little sentence was enough for my little brother to take the rap for it. He tried and tried to convince her that I did it instead of him, but she didn't believe him at all.

One of the things that I am most embarrassed about is peeking at my Christmas gifts. My parents got smart and started hiding most of my presents in the attic, but that didn't happen until much later. They'd put one or two presents under the tree and hide the rest. The first year they hid my gifts, I had no idea. And I was almost in tears by then, because my brother had so many more gifts under the tree than I had. My parents didn't bring down the rest of my presents until we were almost done unwrapping the presents from underneath the tree. I guess I couldn't blame them. I'm not really sure how they found out I had been peeking.

It started out that I'd just peek at my biggest gift that was under the tree. Then it progressed to peeking at whatever I easily could. I'd remove the tape on the end and see what was inside. Then I'd put a new piece of tape on. If the old piece of tape left a mark, I really didn't have to worry about that because mom and dad wouldn't be able to see it. So that's why I think I was so brave. It just seemed so easy. Things got worse, though. Instead of just peeking, I'd carefully open the whole present. If I happened to tear the wrapping or something, I could just re-wrap it. I didn't have to worry about it being re-wrapped with the same type of wrapping paper though, because my parents couldn't see what color the paper was in the first place.

I got so bad that I started opening my presents, using them for a day, and then re-wrapping them. One Christmas, I got a really beautiful sweater. I opened my gift and wore the sweater to school before Christmas. Then the next day, I re-wrapped it and put it back underneath the tree. I can't believe how horrible I was. When Christmas came, there were no surprises. One Christmas, I had peeked at everything that I was getting, and Christmas started to become very disappointing after a while. I'm not sure how my parents figured out that I had been peeking at my gifts. It was probably one of their sighted friends that came over, and noticed that the presents looked like they had been messed with. They never told me outright that they knew, but they did start hiding all my gifts. I was kind of happy that they did, because the surprise of Christmas morning came back.

I didn't just try to get away with things at home. My mom, brother, and I once went over to Josie's house for the weekend. Josie and Ron and their two kids, Anna and Kelly, lived in another town, so we rode the bus. My mom and Josie and Ron would go out, and all of us kids would get to play together. Josie's husband was pretty strict with Anna and Kelly, and always made them finish the food on their plates before they could leave the table. The night we were there, they were having the vegetable I hated the most—peas! My mom didn't make me eat peas at home because she knew that I ate all the other vegetables and she knew I just didn't like peas. But when we were over at Josie and Ron's, Ron thought all the kids should eat their peas. I was pretty upset that we all had to follow Ron's rule and that my mom didn't say no to him. None of us kids liked them. We ate everything on our plates except for the peas, but Ron still wouldn't let us leave the table.

Josie said to just try them, so Anna and Kelly did. But they didn't like them. I came up with a way to trick them. I said, "Okay, I'll try them." I scraped up a spoonful of peas and pretended to put them in my mouth and eat them. I even said, "Oooh, these are good peas. I do like these peas." I pretended to scoop up and eat more. Anna and Kelly and my brother were by then looking at me like I was crazy. They didn't know what I was doing.

After I was done pretending to eat all of the peas, I said, "Those peas were so good, can I get some more?" Ron was smiling. He thought he'd gotten me to eat the peas. I took my plate over to the stove to pretend to get some more peas from the pot. Instead of getting more peas, I dumped my whole plate of peas into the pot. When I came back to the table, I just pretended to eat the second helping of peas. Then I was done. There were no peas on my plate when Ron felt my plate, and I was told I could leave the table. Well, Anna and Kelly followed my lead.

We all got away with it, for a little while at least. My mom was surprised that I had eaten peas. The adults were in shock that we had all liked and eaten our peas. After dinner, when my mom and Josie were cleaning up, I heard Josie tell my mom, "Diane, those girls didn't eat their peas, they put them back into the pan." I heard them laughing about it, too. They thought it was funny that we all tricked Ron. Thank goodness they thought it was funny, because they never did tell Ron, and we didn't get into trouble.

There was one other time we were eating at someone's house and didn't like the food. When we first moved to Vacaville, there was another blind couple that lived there. They heard that my mom and dad were blind and had just moved to town, so they invited us all over for dinner. My mom's brother, who was Uncle Randy to me, had helped us move in, so he was at our house too. My dad was studying, so he didn't go. When the time came, my mom, my brother, Uncle Randy, and I all went over to their house for dinner. They didn't have any kids to play with, so my brother and I were bored. Thank goodness they had dogs to play with. My mom and Uncle Randy visited with the couple for a little while, until the dinner was ready.

We all sat down at the table to eat. The lady had made us cube steak, mashed potatoes, and green beans. It looked delicious, but it wasn't. The meat tasted bad and was hard to chew. It was the worst dinner I had ever tasted. I looked at my brother and Uncle Randy, and they both were making ugly faces about the food too. Thank goodness these people had dogs, and thank goodness they were both blind. I motioned to the dog to come over to the table. I broke my meat up into little pieces and fed it to the dogs. The dogs ate most everything and loved it. I guess they were used to the bad food. We stayed there for a little while after dinner visiting with them, and then we called a taxi to go home. When we all got into the taxi, I confessed to my mom how horrible dinner was and that I had given it to the dogs because I couldn't eat it. I thought my mom would be mad at me. But she actually told me, "I fed mine to the dogs too."

Then my Uncle Randy spoke up and said, "Me too!" We all had given our food to the dogs. The cab ride back home was fun. We were all smiling and laughing because we hadn't realized that each of us had done the same thing. We were all too busy sneaking our own food to the dogs without anyone noticing what everyone else at the table was doing. When we got home, my mom made us something good to eat because we were all still hungry.

The mischief didn't stop when I grew up, either. I was just as bad as a teenager. My mom and I were out grocery shopping once, and I saw the tooth polish and tooth whitener, Pearl Drops, that had been advertised on TV a lot. So I asked my mom if I could get it. She usually said yes to things, but this time she told me no. Well, guess what I did? She couldn't see, so I just put it in the cart anyway. When we got home from the grocery store, I helped put away the groceries. When I found the Pearl Drops, I put them in my pocket and took them to my room. Later that night, I brushed my teeth with my new Pearl Drops. Boy, did my teeth feel good, too. I knew I couldn't let my mom find them, so I put them behind the stack of clothes on the top shelf in my closet. A place I was sure she wouldn't discover them.

The next day, I went to school. When I walked in the door from school, I greeted my mom as I usually did. But something seemed unusual. She was acting a little different than normal. I grabbed a snack from the refrigerator, and went over to my mom who was sitting down in the chair. I asked, "What's wrong, Mom?"

She reached from behind her back, and threw something at me. "Here's your damn Pearl Drops." Busted! Just as I knew that something wasn't quite right when I came home from school that day, my mom had thought something wasn't quite right after we got home from shopping. She thought to herself, "I bet she got the Pearl Drops anyway." So she searched my whole room while I was gone at school. I'm not sure how she found them, or how she even thought to look up in the closet, but she did. My mom was proving wiser than she had ever been before, and she was pretty mad at me for quite a long time for that little deception.

When I became a teenager, I took things to a whole new level. It started when I was about 15 years old. I was a party girl, and there were lots of parties on the weekends. Yes, that meant drinking alcohol too. My mom didn't like the fact that I drank and tried to punish me. But she soon realized that I would just go out and do it anyway. I somehow got away with it. I always tried to hide that I had taken a drink. I used to bring my toothbrush and brush my teeth just before I came home. Mints didn't help either. She always seemed to know what was going on.

My parents were strict about curfews, more so than my friends' parents, so I always had to be home an hour before they would—which I really thought was unfair. They were more lenient with other things than my friends' parents, but not about curfews. No matter how much I begged or pleaded, they wouldn't let me stay out to the same time as my friends. So I started going home early. I'd tell my mom I was tired and going to bed. I'd go into my bedroom and shut the door. A little while later, I'd open my window, jump out, and be back at the party until I wanted to come home.

So after that, when there was a party, my friend would ask her parents if she could spend the night with me. That way, both of us could sneak out the window at my house. It worked out pretty well. We got to stay out as late as we wanted, and my mom and dad were happy that I was home at a decent hour. At least that's what they thought at first. One of my friends, Callie, who was the one I got in the most trouble with, lived in the next town. Her mom was blind too. Sometimes, I'd spend the night at Callie's house, and sometimes she'd spend the night at mine. We'd sneak out at both places, but Callie's house was definitely harder to get back into. The window to her bedroom was much higher.

The first time we sneaked out, Callie had trouble getting back in. I had to jump back out and help her get up to the window. After she was in the window, she also had a hard time getting back down into her room. The first time she tried, she fell and made a loud crash. Her mom came running into the room asking what happened. Thank goodness her mom was blind because we were both standing in her room fully clothed with our jackets still on, when we answered. "Oh, Callie just fell out of bed." Her mom was worried that she was hurt, but we both said that she was okay. Callie's mom went back into her room and back to bed. The next morning Callie's mom asked if Callie was okay, but that was it. So

Callie and I had gotten away with sneaking out her window, too.

A couple of weeks later, I was spending the night at Callie's house again. We came home early from being out on Saturday night. We went to her bedroom and stayed quiet for about an hour before sneaking out the window. When we finally came back, it was the same thing again. Callie couldn't get in. So I helped her and then climbed in myself. This time, Callie didn't fall inside her room. We were whispering and joking how easy this was. Then Callie reached over to turn on the light. Uh-oh, Callie's mom was standing in the corner of her room with her arms crossed, tapping her foot. She was mad, very mad. In fact, her mom had been waiting for us to return for a few hours by then. Of course, Callie's mom told my mom, and that was the last time that Callie and I could sneak out together. Thank goodness my mom got less strict about my curfew as I got a few years older. I think that her reasoning was that she would rather know that I was out and going to come home later than be deceived into thinking I was safely home when I wasn't.

One of the worst things I did—something I'm not very proud to have done—was when my friend Tani and I were out partying. She came back home with me to spend the night. We were pretty drunk when we got home, too. My mom and dad were already in bed. So at first, we were trying to be quiet. Then we started thinking about the joke we had heard earlier in the day. It was a Hellen Keller joke, so it was funny because my parents were blind. I thought it was hilarious:

How did Hellen Keller's parents punish her?
They moved the furniture without telling her.

So, when Tani and I got home, we thought it would be funny

to move the furniture. We rearranged the sofa, the coffee table, and one of the chairs in the living room. The next morning, my mom started walking down the hallway toward the living room, and *boom*. She ran straight into the sofa. Then she banged her shin into the coffee table trying to get around the sofa. She was mad. I think she was a little hurt by what we did, too. Tani and I moved the furniture back. But I felt really stupid and guilty the rest of the day. My mom was pretty mad about it for quite a while.

My brother was never like me. He actually took after my mom a lot. Unfortunately—for my parents anyway—I took after my dad. I guess that's why I got into so much trouble. I was just like him when he was younger. My brother hardly did anything bad, and when he did, it was mild compared to the trouble that I caused my parents. When my brother was probably seven or eight years old, he stole some quarters out of my mother's purse so he could go to the store and buy candy. Well, my mom noticed that the quarters were missing, and she knew it wasn't me that time, because I had been gone all weekend. So it was definitely my brother. When she asked him, he readily confessed to doing it. My mom was so hurt that her sweet little boy stole from her that she cried. She couldn't believe that her good son did something like that. It was the first time that he had ever done anything bad.

Then, when my brother was a teenager, he tried smoking. He was pretty stupid in how he went about it, though. It wasn't like he was off with his friends behind some building, or out in the orchard where the other kids smoked. Oh, no. He tried smoking in our house while he was taking a shower. He'd open the window and hold the cigarette next to the window, so that the smoke would go outside. But what he *didn't* do was remember to remove the cigarette butt off the windowsill after he got out of the shower. My mom found it one day when she was cleaning. He would have gotten away with it if he had just taken the cigarette butt with him and thrown it in the trash. Not a very well thought-out plan.

That was the extent of what my brother did his whole life growing up. He was always the good kid and almost never did anything wrong. I, on the other hand, looked for trouble and trouble looked for me. I was always trying to get away with things, or trying to figure out a way around the rules. I guess I made up for my brother being so good, because I caused enough trouble for the both of us. I don't think I would have been any different if my parents weren't blind, but I definitely took advantage of the fact that they were at every opportunity that I could. I guess my brother and I were pretty typical kids, just like in any other family. My brother and I had distinct and different personalities just like any other kids. My parents just took it one day at a time and dealt with us however they saw best, just like any other parent has to do. Raising kids is never exactly what any parent expects it will be.

Chapter 10
Things That Only Happen in a Blind Family

THERE WERE SOME THINGS THAT HAPPENED IN our family that could have happened to anyone in any family. And sometimes the things that happened were pretty scary, too. They are incidents that come up so quickly that a person really doesn't have very much time to think about them—no time to make a plan—but instead, just sort of react to the immediate issue at hand. Well, a couple of these situations came up for my parents, and my dad reacted like the protector that he was. He couldn't see, but he sure did move into action as quickly as he could to protect all of us. The ways that my parents handled emergencies were probably a little different approaches other, sighted parents might have taken.

When we lived in Hayward, our apartment was two stories. The living room, dining room, and kitchen were downstairs, along with a small bathroom, a coat closet, and a small, enclosed patio. Our bedrooms and a bathroom were upstairs. We had lived in that apartment for a few years, starting when I was about six or seven years old. Late one night, my dad woke me up and whispered to me to be quiet and follow him. I didn't know why. I just did it. Then he whispered in my ear that we were going to go quietly downstairs, because he thought someone was in our apartment. I was supposed to stay crouched between his legs, and I wasn't supposed to get in front of him. Again, I wasn't totally sure what we were doing, but I trusted and obeyed my dad.

He then grabbed my hand with one of his as I ducked between his legs just like he said. He was holding a baseball bat with his other hand. He whispered to me again when we were partway downstairs: "I'm going to turn on a light, and when I ask I want you to scream as loudly as you can if you see anyone. Scream and let me know where the person is. Then I want you to dart back between my legs and get behind me as quickly as you can, so I don't accidentally hit you. Your mom is upstairs listening, so she can call the police if she has to."

So we quietly went all the way downstairs. My dad flipped on the light, but no one was there. So we walked over to the closet, and my dad quickly swung open the door. "Dad, no one is in there." Then we walked over to the bathroom door and he swung open that door. "Dad, no one is in there." What a relief. Thank goodness no one had broken into our apartment. My dad then told me to go back upstairs while he checked all the doors and windows to make sure they remained locked. Then he came upstairs and went back to bed himself.

That night, my dad was going to protect us, but he needed me to be his eyes to do it. That was one of the scariest things that I had ever done for my dad. I really didn't think about it. I just obeyed. I am just thankful that no one was in our apartment. I'm not sure that my dad would have done it the same way if he had to do it over again. It happened so quickly, and he reacted the best way that he knew how. He trusted me to be his eyes.

There was one other situation that came up that was pretty scary, and my dad jumped into action again, in spite of not having the advantage of sight. It was the middle of the night. I woke up to smoke filling my room, and found I couldn't breathe very well. I opened my bedroom door and could barely see my dad through the smoke. He was running into the bathroom with something in his arms, and screaming for my mom to get out of his way. I didn't know what was going on. I knew something was burning, but it was too frantic when I opened the door to make sense of the scene. Then I heard fire engines, and knew we were safe. The firemen came running into our house.

As it turns out, the electric blanket had caught on fire. My mom ran to the phone in the kitchen to call the fire department. My dad reacted as quickly as he could, and did the only thing that came to his mind to effectively stop the fire from spreading. He grabbed the burning bedding into his arms, without knowing the extent of the flames of course, and ran into the bathroom to throw it into the bathtub, the safest and closest place he knew to contain that fire. He turned on the shower to put out the flames.

When the firemen came into the house, there was thick smoke throughout our house. When they ran into the bedroom, the only thing they saw was a smoldering mattress. They grabbed a fire extinguisher from their truck, and made sure the mattress wasn't burning anymore. The firemen were a little baffled by how much smoke was in the house, and what little evidence of fire they had seen in the bedroom. That's when my dad stepped out of the bathroom. My dad told them what he had done with the electric blanket. They were shocked. They told him that was one of the smartest things he could have thought to do. They removed all the blankets from the bathtub to make sure the fire was out. They also walked around the house to ensure there was nothing else burning, and then they left.

What they didn't see, and what they didn't know, was how badly burned my dad was. His hands and arms were red and blistered, but the firemen had been so shocked and stunned by what my dad had done with all the bedding, they'd never thought to ask him if he was physically okay. The next day, his burns were so painful that he went to the doctor. He had second degree burns covering his hands and arms, but he said it was all worth it so that his house didn't burn down and everyone else was safe.

Most of the quirky and memorable things that happened in our family could really only happen in a household with blind parents. There are just some things that are unique that would never happen in families where the adults were sighted. They were by far not nearly as dramatic and scary as the fire or possible intruder stories. Some of these are even a little funny because they were unexpected.

Heiress was my mom's first guide dog. Guide dogs are raised and socialized by 4-H members and their families for a year, and then given to Guide Dogs for the Blind, an organization that trains each dog for approximately a year. When each dog is about two years old, a blind person goes to the school and trains with it. They learn how to take care of their dog, its feeding schedule, how to walk with their guide dog in public, and about the laws regarding working with guide dogs and accompaniment in public places, for example.

So by the time my mom trained with Heiress, the dog was already two years old. When my mom brought her home, Heiress was always eager to work and go out walking. Every time my mom would get Heiress's leash and harness, Heiress would come running. After about six or seven years, Heiress got a little slower. When she wasn't excited to go out anymore, my mom retired her from service. All that meant is that Heiress just stayed at home with us to live her life as a pet, like any regular dog. After Heiress was retired, my mom went back to Guide Dogs for the Blind to get another guide dog to work with, so she could get around town and run her errands.

My mom's second guide dog was Karo. Heiress and Karo were pals, and every time my mom would get out the dog harness and leash for Karo to go for a walk, Heiress would get up and wag her tail and want to come. It hurt my mom to see Heiress so sad when she and Karo left the house and left poor Heiress behind. So the next time my mom went out walking with Karo, she let Heiress out to walk behind them. Heiress was a much happier dog after that. Heiress would walk behind, but she somehow knew that she wasn't working, so she stopped and sniffed at everything she wanted, something a working guide dog can never do. When my mom would get to an intersection, she'd call Heiress to make sure they all crossed the street together.

Sometimes, my mom would walk around the neighborhood just to give the dogs some exercise. Other times she would walk down to the convenience store a few blocks away. When my mom opened the door to go into the convenience store, Heiress wandered right inside the store too. Heiress didn't know that she wasn't supposed to go in while she wasn't working, since she had always gone in before, when she was in service. So my mom just let her, and the owner of the store didn't mind.

Each time my mom and Karo went out for their walk down to the store, Heiress was right behind them. One day, just as many times before, my mom went to the store and walked back home with the dogs. My mom took the harness and leash off of Karo, and reached down to pet Heiress at the same time. Well, my mom was surprised to find that Heiress had something in her mouth. So my mom took hold of it to find out what it was. It was a whole loaf of bread. Heiress had grabbed a loaf of bread from the store, and was just holding it in her mouth, wagging her tail the whole time. The clerk at the store had said goodbye to my mom as always, but didn't say a word when Heiress walked out with bread hanging from her mouth. After that, my mom stopped letting Heiress into the store. Instead, Heiress waited patiently outside for them to come out.

What my mom didn't realize was that when Heiress was following behind off leash, she wasn't just sniffing at things. She was also pooping in other people's yards, which of course is terribly impolite for a pet. My mom would always let Heiress out in the backyard before she went on her walks, so she wouldn't have to stop when they were out walking, but I guess Heiress liked other people's yards better. One day, my mom heard a knock on the door. She opened the door, but no one answered, so she walked outside and felt around on the porch. Someone had left a bag. She reached inside to see what they had left. Well, some nasty person had scooped up all the dog poop from their yard and left it for my mom. My mom never found out which neighbor did it, but she tried to be more careful afterwards, at least making sure Heiress had gone potty before going out for her walk.

My mom had a total of four guide dogs. The first three of them were Golden Retrievers: Heiress, Karo, and Fonda. Her last dog was Josette, a black Labrador. All the names were picked out by the school, and each dog was specifically matched for my mom based on my mom's personality and the personality of the dog. They were all wonderful dogs and family pets that made wonderful companions for all of my mom's travels. All of them have long passed away, but are still lovingly remembered by all of us.

Figure 25: Graduation ceremony at Guide Dogs for the Blind in San Rafael, CA. Left to right: Guide Dogs for the Blind representative, my mom and Josette, and the 4-H volunteer who raised Josette from a puppy.

Sometimes, we did things a certain way because it was easier. Since we didn't have a car, lots of times I'd ride my bike down to the store to pick up something for dinner that we had forgotten to get. Sometimes, I'd even ride my bike to a restaurant to pick up some takeout food if my mom didn't feel like cooking, or if we were having a treat. I'm sure most kids did things like this. But sometimes, what my parents really wanted was a bottle of alcohol so they could have a drink with dinner. I couldn't buy it myself, of course, because I was too young. My mom didn't want to call a taxi to go to the liquor store either. "What would the taxi driver think if I called him to just go buy a bottle of booze?" she'd say.

So instead, I'd ride my mom to the liquor store on the back of my bike. She'd sit on my bicycle seat and hold onto me while I stood up and pedaled to the store, which was about a mile away. Then she'd hold onto the bottle of liquor in the bag with one hand, and hold onto me with her other hand on the return trip home. We'd ride to the liquor store through a park and along two busy roads. My mom really trusted me, it seems, because I don't think many parents would trust their ten-year-old daughter to ride them on the back of their bike, especially down to the store in traffic like that.

As I mentioned before, my mom was pretty graceful as she walked around our house. She knew the layout of our house so well, she would walk from one room to the other without hesitation, just like a sighted person. One summer day, she was reading her Braille book in the breeze that always came through the screen doors. Someone knocked on the front door, so she got up and went to the door. The guy at the door saw my mom walk around the corner, and he started to introduce himself. He said that he was just out of high school trying to raise money to go to college, and was selling magazines. He held up his list of magazines for my mom to look at.

My mom responded that she was sorry, but could not buy any magazines because she was blind and could not read them. Well, my mom doesn't look blind at all. When my mom gets up in the morning, she puts in prosthetic eyes every day. So her eyes look just like the eyes of a sighted person at first glance. If you really studied my mom, you would realize that even though her prosthetic eyes move and look real at first, her eyes don't focus, and it seems they just kind of blankly stare into nothingness. Well, this young gentleman did not believe her. He said, "I watched you walk to the door. You looked right at me, and when I held up my magazine list, you looked right at it." My mom tried to convince him that she was blind, but he never believed her. He went as far as to call my mom a liar, and told her that was the worst excuse that anyone had ever told him. He was mad when he left, and stormed off to the next house. My mom walked back into the living room chuckling a bit, sat down, and continued to read her Braille book like nothing had happened.

My mom's first prosthetic eye covered the eye that got pushed in when she ran into the sink as a little girl. She used to keep her eye in the cupboard, in a cup of water that kept it moist overnight. She would rinse it off and then put it in most every morning. Every night at bedtime, her eye would go back into the cup with fresh water. Once a year or so, she would have to take her eye in to get it polished. There were some days that her eye was hurting so much that she didn't want to wear it, but there weren't very many of those days. Every few years, her body would change, or the prosthetic eye would become uncomfortable, and she'd eventually get a new one.

When I was in school, I used my mom's eye as a conversation piece, mostly to freak out the other kids. I'd sometimes tell the other kids something like, "My mom can take her eye out." They all thought I was lying, of course. I'd sometimes tell them, "She keeps her eye in a cup of water in the cupboard." But they didn't really believe me. When they didn't believe me, I'd tell them to come over to my house and see. Some of the kids were too scared to come over, freaked out that they really would see an eyeball in a cup of water. That wasn't a normal event at their houses!

My mom was a little embarrassed when I brought home a kid from school and the first thing I would ask was, "Mom, you can take your eye out?" But she was a pretty good sport about it. I think she even showed one of my friends that she could. And sometimes, my mom wouldn't be wearing her eye at all, so they'd get to see it resting in the cup of water.

I'm not sure why my mom kept her eye in the cupboard. It was in the same cupboard as the empty glasses we would use for our drinks, but the glass with her eye in it was kept higher up on a different shelf. There were a lot of times that people would ask if they could get themselves a glass of water and then ask where the cups were. When they opened the cupboard, they would sometimes get the surprise of their life seeing the cup with the eye. We could always tell when they saw it, too, because they would be happily talking and then it would be total silence.

My mom kept pretty good track of her eye. There was only one time that she set the cup down and couldn't remember where she put it. She didn't want my dad to accidentally knock it over and lose the eye on the floor, so my brother scoured the whole house looking for it.

My mom had called the Fire Department because the electricity had gone out with a boom. She was told to call them by the utility company because she was blind, so they would check to see what the problem was. After all, that was the fastest resource just in case something was wrong. They came a lot faster than she had expected, so after she answered the door, she took her eye into the bathroom to put it in—without the firemen seeing her do it. She rinsed it off and was just getting ready to put it in, when it slipped right out of her hand. She heard it bounce. It took two bounces on the bathroom counter, and then there was a little plop—and a splash. Of course, it landed in the worst place possible: *the toilet.*

She left the bathroom and told one of the firemen, "Oh, by the way, I've got another problem now." She explained that her prosthetic eye fell into the toilet, and asked if they could get it out for her. A fireman looked into the toilet, and saw her eye—way in the back of the bowl where it couldn't be reached. So he grabbed a hanger and tried to move it to the front of the bowl so that he could reach in and grab it . . . but he pushed it the wrong way. Instead, it went down. He was sorry. My mom had to order a new eye. She was kind of glad that it wasn't recovered, because she really didn't want to put the eye that that had been in the toilet back in her socket. A few weeks later, she had a brand new eye.

A lot later in life, when my dad was in his 40s or 50s, he developed traumatic onset glaucoma from the trauma that his eyes suffered in the accident that caused him to be blind. Both my mom and dad starting having pain in their eyes from the pressure caused by their glaucoma, and they each decided to have their natural eyes surgically removed around that time. So at that point, my mom and dad each had two prosthetic eyes.

My dad didn't like to wear his eyes. It was hard to get used to having them in. When he would wear them, it was only when he went out in public. Then he stopped even doing that, and would just wear his dark glasses while he was in public. My mom was always telling him, "Roy, can you put your eyes in? Someone is coming over." Sometimes he would—and sometimes he wouldn't. It was a little gross to see him without his glasses, as I bet there aren't too many people that know or can even imagine what an empty eye socket actually looks like. But I can. It isn't a pretty sight, either. The only way to explain it is if you can imagine what your flesh would look like if you peeled your skin back. It's raw, and bloody-looking. It looks like it should be bleeding, but it isn't. It is shiny and moist. It is purely and simply yucky! Something you really don't want to see even if you have a chance, and certainly very startling if you are not accustomed to seeing one from time to time.

In addition to not having eyes, my dad had his teeth pulled and got dentures when he was a little older. It was really not a pretty sight to see him without his *eyes and* without his teeth. But being the jokester that he was, he'd sometimes come out of the bedroom like that. Little kids from the neighborhood thought he was a monster and were horrified. My dad would just laugh when he scared the kids. He thought it was funny. The little kids were so scared that they didn't want to ever come back to our house.

Some of the things that happened to our family were out of our control. People were always putting our names in for something that was usually well-meaning but sometimes a little embarrassing. My mom and dad would get calls all the time for things that we had won, and wonder how, because no one in our family entered the drawing or contest involved. When my parents would ask who had put their names in, no one seemed to know. So every so often, we would get random calls for our address in order for something to get mailed to us, or have to go pick something up. It was never anything very big, but sometimes it was a little hassle, or maybe a bit awkward.

One time, our name was put in for something we never expected. I was nine and my brother was five years old, and we were spending our first Christmas in our new house in Vacaville. We had just finished opening all of our gifts, and were clearing away all the wrapping paper when we heard the sirens. It sounded like fire trucks, and the sirens were really close, so we knew they had stopped somewhere on our street. My mom said, "I hope our neighbors don't have a fire on Christmas." We soon learned that was not what was going on at all. Suddenly, we heard a very forceful knock on our front door. "Fire Department," they said. My brother and I were looking at each other, a little confused. I know that I was thinking, "We don't have a fire. Why is the Fire Department at our house?" My mom knew, though. She told us to quickly hide the presents. We were trying to put away the presents, when my mom opened the door.

The firemen barged quickly into our house, yelling, "Merry Christmas. Ho, Ho, Ho!" One of them was dressed like Santa Claus, and they had gifts, too. I didn't know what was going on, but my parents did. As fast as they came in, the firemen left the house. They left my brother and I pretty stunned, but we were happy because we had more presents.

There were a few huge bags of used toys, and a faded old wagon that turned out to have one wobbly wheel. We opened the bags, and they were each full of other kids' used toys. Some of them were even broken. The dolls didn't have clothes, and some of the toys were dirty. But there were also some new toys in there, too. We ended up throwing away some of the really old toys that we didn't want. What was really funny is that my mom and dad had bought us a brand new wagon that year. So we had one shiny new wagon, and one faded wagon with a wobbly wheel. The second wagon came in handy for wagon races with our friends.

We found out later that one of my dad's ham radio friends submitted our family's name for the charitable Christmas because my parents were blind. We weren't the first blind people in Vacaville, but we were the first blind family, and that was good enough to make it to the top of the Fire Department's list of needy people. I know that I was embarrassed, and so were my parents. But we all smiled and simply hoped it wouldn't happen again next year. The next Christmas we were all on the alert, and thought that we would just pretend we weren't home and not answer the door if they came again. Thank goodness the Fire Department never showed up for any more of our Christmases.

The good thing about the Fire Department bringing us gifts was that no one really knew about it. It wasn't announced in the paper and none of our friends knew it had happened. My parents were the most embarrassed, because they knew better than we kids did what it really meant—someone assumed that they were really poor and couldn't afford to buy their kids any gifts. But they were gracious just like they always were, and told my dad's ham friend thank you, because they knew he did it out of kindness and nothing else.

People have always tried to help my parents without asking if help was needed, so my parents just kind of got used to it and would always be gracious that someone thought of them. My brother and I were never usually aware of everything that was being done for them unless it was blatant, like the Fire Department coming to our house on Christmas. So what people did for my parents, or for us, never really affected us much. We would think of them as perks and be happy about them too. It was a choice to approach every gesture as kindness. No matter what was happening with us, it just always seemed to work itself out.

Chapter 11
The Judgment of It All

BEING BLIND ISN'T EASY, EVEN THOUGH MY parents made it look easy most of the time. Friends and family knew how well my parents did things, and they were usually humbled by the fact that my parents could function just as well as the rest of us who were sighted. But there were some things my parents didn't have any control over, and that certainly included other people's actions, or how other people treated them and our family. Along with all the good things and the fun times our family had, there were some darker moments too. My parents didn't dwell on the negative or lament what they didn't have control over. They just moved on from disappointments and tried not to let others' actions impact their lives too much.

My mom and dad always had trouble finding places to live. They had trouble when they were a young married couple on their own and even later, when we were a family. It wasn't as commonplace to see a blind or disabled person out in public in the 1960s and 1970s as it is today. Families would keep disabled people at home because they always needed to be taken care of. Most people were just not accustomed to seeing independent blind people, and unless they knew a blind person more intimately, a lot of people just didn't think they could handle it. That was the mentality back then, but unfortunately, it is still prevalent today.

Apartment managers didn't want to rent to a blind couple, because they thought even a *single* blind person would be too much hassle. Apartment managers thought they would need to babysit them because they would always need extra help. So when my mom and dad went out in search of new places to live, they were commonly told that there were no apartments available to rent, even though they had called beforehand and, before mentioning any disability, may have been told there were several. When the manager saw that they were blind, apartments suddenly became "unavailable," and the complex had "no vacancies."

Other times, my parents were told that they were thought an insurance risk, because the managers didn't think that my parents would be safe living alone. They often assumed that my parents would be a constant bother and burden to them, so they refused. My parents were even refused places to live because managers thought they wouldn't or couldn't pay the required rent. There are probably a lot more reasons that the managers thought were "valid," but it all boiled down to discrimination.

Looking for a place to live wasn't the only form of discrimination that my parents endured. Whenever my mom and I would go out shopping, it turned into an all-day event. We'd have to take buses and that meant we had to wait for buses, too. So we'd be gone most of the day, and that usually meant we'd have to stop someplace and eat lunch. Most of the time we ate at the same places because they were familiar, and close to the stores where we usually shopped. But sometimes we had to search for a new place to eat because we weren't as familiar with the area. Before we ordered, my mom would have me look at the menu to make sure there was something on the menu that we both liked. Having me look at the menu beforehand started when I first learned my alphabet, and I'd have to spell everything on the menu to my mom. It got easier as I actually learned to read, of course. Sometimes, we'd go into a restaurant or diner and end up walking right out because there didn't seem to be anything we wanted to eat on the menu.

One day, we stopped into a new café, and my mom and I sat at the counter. The menu was on the counter, so I started looking through it. When I saw it was a good place to eat, I told my mom, "Mama, they have a lot of things that we can eat here."

The manager of the cafe came over to my mom and was talking to her, and the next thing that my mom said was: "Come on, Laura, let's go find someplace else to eat."

"No, Mama, they have good things to eat here." The more that I tried to convince her that it was a good place to eat, the more forceful she became, saying we needed to leave at once. I didn't understand at first, because she always left it up to me to make sure the menu had something good for us to eat. We quietly walked out of there, and never returned. What I didn't realize as a kid was that the owner of the diner approached and actually told my mom that he would not serve us. It was only later that I realized that we were being kicked out of the restaurant because my mom was blind.

The discrimination even happened when we were with other sighted people. My aunt, my mom, and I had been eating at a restaurant inside a department store where we had been shopping.

When we finished eating and the bill came, we left the money on the table with a tip as we had always done. We then grabbed our shopping bags and walked out of the store, finished for the day. We were already over a block away heading to the bus stop when an out-of-breath man from the department store told us to return to the store. We didn't know why, so we walked all the way back.

When we arrived at the store, the manager accused us of not paying for our meal, and told us that we needed to pay or they would call the police. When my mom told the manager that we left the money on the table, he said that he didn't believe us because "someone had looked." My aunt walked all the way back to the restaurant and showed him where we had put the money. To his surprise, it was right on the table—just like we had said. We were able to go then, but with no apologies. Things like this happened all the time to us.

For some reason, people assumed that blind people just don't have any money and couldn't or wouldn't pay. On many occasions, when we walked into a store or restaurant, we were asked, "Are you sure you have the money to pay?" We even had to pay upfront for our meals at times because restaurant staff assumed we would not pay. Even after my parents would tell them that they had money, we would sometimes be watched while shopping because someone at a store thought that we were going to steal. I'd sometimes notice and observe, "Mama, that man is following us." My mom was used to things like this happening and she would just tell me to ignore, it which I rarely could. I was too young to actually know why he was following us, so I would just stare back at him while he was watching my mom.

The discrimination happened sometimes when it was least expected, too. My dad had been riding both Greyhound buses and local city buses by himself ever since he became blind and learned mobility at the blind school. My dad once joined my mom, my brother, and I on our yearly summer trip to stay at my grandma and grandpa's house in Southern California. My dad usually didn't come with us because he would take classes all throughout the year. This time, though, he took a short break and took the trip, but would have to return early for school.

We all rode the Greyhound bus for the long 12- to 14-hour trip. The usual six-hour drive in a car took much longer by bus, because the bus had to stop at all the bus stations along the way. My mom and dad scheduled an evening departure, so all of us could sleep on the bus for most of the trip. When we'd get to our destination, Grandma Ione and Grandpa Woody always met us at the bus station. It was always fun going to their house each summer, because they would take us some place big while we were visiting. Some of the attractions were Disneyland, Universal Studios, and Knott's Berry Farm, places that we hadn't been to.

My dad had to leave earlier than we did because he had to get back home in time for the start of summer classes. My grandpa took him to the Greyhound bus station and waited with him until the bus came. When the bus pulled up, the driver got out and stood by the door taking tickets from the new passengers getting on the bus. My grandpa and my dad walked over to give the driver my dad's ticket so my dad could board the bus, but the driver refused the ticket. He told my grandpa, "I don't want to babysit him on my bus." As much as my dad tried to convince him that he was independent and didn't need any help, the bus driver stood his ground and wouldn't let him board.

The Greyhound bus that my dad had bought a ticket for pulled out of the station without him. When my dad went inside to complain about what had just happened and to see when the next bus was leaving, the station manager told my dad, "Bus drivers have the right to refuse anyone who they think is incapable of taking care of himself." My dad asked about the next bus, and the station manager told him that the next driver might do the same thing—that there were no guarantees he could ride on the next bus, either.

So my dad ended up having to get a ride to the airport, take a plane back home to Northern California, and then find a way home from the airport after he landed. My dad was angry, and wrote several letters to Greyhound. He said that he had been discriminated against, but no one at Greyhound responded to any of his letters. My dad contacted several attorneys so that he could file a discrimination lawsuit against Greyhound, but each attorney told him, "It isn't worth it. Greyhound will countersue and it will get messy." So my dad was on his own to fight this. My dad and some our family friends continued to call and write letters about the incident that happened on May 20, 1970. Finally, over a year later and after many subsequent calls and letters from many people to Greyhound about the matter, Greyhound finally responded:

As I Saw It

Roy
Steve

GREYHOUND LINES—WEST

371 Market Street
San Francisco, CA 94106
(415) 362-4664

August 4, 1971

Mr. S. C. Furman
396 Teddy Drive
Union City, California 94587

Dear Mr. Furman:

    This is in reference to our telephone conversation and subsequent correspondence concerning an incident involving your blind friend, Mr. Roy Phelps.

    Please forgive the delay in replying to your letter of June 22nd, however, it was necessary that I trace our Los Angeles office for information concerning their handling of the incident, in addition to my being absent from the office on business frequently during the month of July.

    It is noted that Mr. Phelps' complaint was called to our attention by the Public Utilities Commission on May 26, 1970, and an investigation was conducted by our Los Angeles Regional Manager, and corrective action was taken with the driver and other employees involved.

    As a result of this complaint, Greyhound employees, both salaried and commissioned agents, were reinstructed concerning the handling of blind passengers. Our employees were instructed concerning our tariff responsibility to sell tickets to blind passengers as well as our moral responsibility to see that these people are aided while in our depots and on and off our buses.

    I feel confident, Mr. Furman, that as a result of Mr. Phelps' complaint, all of our employees have been and will continue doing a much improved job in handling not only blind passengers but all those who are handicapped as well.

    Thank you again for bringing this matter to my attention, and if further information is desired please let me know.

                                              Very truly yours,

                                              G. E. Barnhart
                                            Asst. to Vice President - Traffi

GEB:pv

Greyhound didn't really apologize to my dad, but nonetheless my dad was satisfied that he did what he could about the situation. My dad just wanted to make sure that this didn't happen again to him or to anyone else. He was glad that Greyhound had finally acknowledged that the discrimination had taken place, and had instructed their employees not to let something like this happen again.

Sometimes the scenario wasn't strictly discrimination; it was other, ordinary people simply taking advantage of the fact that my parents were blind. For example, my mom and dad had no problem feeling the difference between coins. It was the bill denominations they had trouble with, because they are all the same size and felt the same to them. Whenever my mom or dad would come home from a store or any other place having been given paper money as change, I would have to sit down with them and tell them what denomination the bills were. I'd tell them what each bill was, and they'd fold each stack differently so they wouldn't have to rely on anyone to know their money.

A kid came to our apartment once selling candy bars, after my mom had gone to the bank and before her money was folded and put away. My mom decided to buy two candy bars from the kid to help out his school, so she grabbed a bill from her wallet and asked the boy if it was a $1 bill. He said that it was one dollar. My mom asked him two or three times during the transaction, just to be sure she was giving him the correct amount, and each time he said that it was a $1 that she had. So my mom asked for two candy bars and handed the dollar bill to him in payment.

I came home from school just a little later, and then I sat down with my mom to go over her money and fold it. That's when she discovered that the bill she had given the kid selling candy wasn't a $1 bill after all. It was a $20 bill. So she called the police. The police found the boy and told his parents that he had lied to a blind lady and effectively stolen from her. The police brought the boy back to our house, made him apologize to my mom, and give back the $20 he had dishonestly taken. The kid was in trouble with his parents, too. I was only about seven when this happened, and was happy that we ended up keeping the candy bars and getting all our money back. I wasn't sure why my parents weren't as happy about getting "free" candy back then, but now realize how they must have felt to be the object of theft from a neighborhood child. This incident was small, but there were many other people that my parents encountered who also tried to cheat them when I wasn't around to watch out for them.

My dad suffered four distinct tragedies in his lifetime. The first tragedy was the accident he suffered being burned and going blind. The second tragedy was the hit-and-run accident that broke his leg. The third was getting gangrene in his injured leg and almost having it amputated. But it was the fourth tragedy that affected me the most, because by this time I was old enough to watch it happen. Over time, I got to see how it actually impacted and affected my dad, and saw the toll it took on him before he was able to move on with his life. In some ways, it was the worst tragic development of his whole life.

After much struggle and a lot of time invested, my dad finished school. He was so proud that he was able to get back on his feet after going blind and after the hit-and-run accident. He worked hard through school, ultimately completing his master's degree in Rehabilitation Counseling. It was hard for him, but through perseverance and dedication, he graduated with honors. My dad sacrificed time with our family because he wanted to be able to support us on his own, but he also had a very strong desire and purpose to be able to help others that had been through tragic ordeals just as he had. He just wanted to help and be able to show people how to overcome and continue on with life like he had learned some time before. But he had to do that, too, in a different way than he would have expected.

My dad started pursuing jobs during the semester before he graduated. He applied and interviewed at several places in Sacramento because he knew how to get around in that area using the bus system. He wanted to work in a place where he could commute from our established home, so our family wasn't disrupted. Going to interviews wasn't easy on him, since it required that he take Greyhound buses, city buses, and sometimes even taxis to get to the interview locations, just like he did to get to campus. If interviews were early in the morning, he'd get near the location the night before and sleep in a hotel. When he couldn't find a job locally, he started looking outside the area.

My dad submitted resumes all over the state. Every time he had an interview, he had to figure out how to get there using the buses and taxis, and most of the time, it wasn't easy. Sometimes, he took Greyhound and local buses, but occasionally he had to fly to the interviews. After a few years of applying, taking tests, and interviewing for positions without offers of work, my dad gave up trying to get a job in Rehabilitation Counseling. In the 1970s, there weren't yet any laws protecting the blind or the disabled from discrimination, and no one wanted to hire a blind man for this job. My dad scored very high on the skill and aptitude tests he took for the positions he applied for, but that still wasn't enough.

Before 1962, disabled people weren't allowed to go to college and get an education. It was only after a disabled man sued for that right—and won—that disabled people were considered at all, but there was still discrimination in place everywhere because the lawsuit filed in 1962 was the first of its kind. It took over 11 years to enact federal law protecting disabled people, effectively guaranteeing their right to go to college at all. This was initiated in the Rehabilitation Act of 1973 (Section 504), but it was only for federally funded institutions:

> "No otherwise qualified handicapped individual in the United States, shall, solely by reason of his [sic] handicap, be excluded from the participation in, be denied the benefits of, or be subjected to discrimination under any program or activity receiving federal financial assistance."
> https://en.m.wikipedia.org/wiki/Timeline_of_disability_rights_in_the_United_States

It wasn't until as late as 1990, when the Federal Americans with Disabilities Act (ADA) was enacted, that people with disabilities were guaranteed equal rights to live the whole scope of their lives like any other person. The ADA provided:

[C]omprehensive civil rights protection for people with disabilities. Closely modeled after the Civil Rights Act and Section 504, the law was the most sweeping disability rights legislation in American history. It mandated that local, state, and federal governments and programs be accessible, that employers with more than 15 employees make "reasonable accommodations" for workers with disabilities and not discriminate against otherwise qualified workers with disabilities, and that public accommodations and commercial facilities make "reasonable modifications" to ensure access for disabled members of the public, and not discriminate against them. It also mandated provision of disabled-access toilet facilities in private buildings.

Unfortunately for my dad, these laws were enacted a little too late for him, at least in terms of his career. But his story is probably like many others who tried to achieve such goals before society actually caught up to protect the many that had been discriminated against. Even though my dad wasn't able to get a job in his field, his life went on. Just as the accident that left him blind didn't stop him, neither did this setback. He kept busy and made a happy life for himself and his family. He did what he could under the circumstances and didn't let what was out of his control stop him from living.

Both my parents lived their lives using this philosophy. When things happened to them, they moved on. They didn't dwell on them. They would take action wherever possible, but also live with the outcome if it didn't work. They learned to move on because they had to. Society wasn't always so nice, but they persevered through the bad and made a wonderful life for themselves and our family, however adapted, in ways other people wouldn't think to do.

Chapter 12
Fulfilled Lives, Keeping Busy

MY PARENTS WERE VERY ACTIVE IN THE local chapter of the blind club, Solano County Council of the Blind, which my mom still attends. My dad was president for a couple of years, and my mom was secretary for many of those years and president for a year herself. At the chapter meetings, they would discuss current issues and laws affecting blind and disabled people, and encouraged the members to get involved with activism for their own rights. The members also discussed what the local county and city governments were doing for the blind and disabled.

The president also was responsible for conveying the agendas of both the state organization, California Council of the Blind, and the national organization, American Council of the Blind. There were always new programs for the disabled, new products, or some new gadgets that had just come out for them to learn about. The officers of the blind club would therefore attend the yearly state convention and sometimes go to the national conventions.

It seemed that my mom and dad were always going to blind conventions. The state conventions were held in large hotels in cities, where they would have meetings, discussions, and events for all the attendees in the different rooms of the hotel. The conventions would have classes on the new technology and even hold demonstrations for new devices, usually delivered by the companies that created the devices. There were meetings and discussions about current laws and regulations that affected the blind, along with previews of legislation that was currently being written.

There would be travel agents talking about the vacations they had created to be marketed to disabled, especially blind persons. If there was something that was helpful or might be interesting to a blind person, it usually had a representative at these conventions. During a convention, of course, the hotel was mainly booked with blind people and would hire extra people to assist the attendees if they needed. There were hundreds of blind members from all over the state, getting around by cane or guide dog, being assisted by a sighted person, or wandering around the hotel by themselves using cues learned, presumably, in mobility training.

Once, I went to the hotel to pick up my mom from one of the conventions she attended. Often, when I needed to pick up my mom and couldn't find her right away, I could just ask if anyone had seen a blind lady around—and I'd be able to find my mom. But not at this place! Everyone was blind but the hotel staff. I saw blind people hanging onto other blind people to get around. Every place I walked, I had to avoid bumping into a blind person. I was amazed and also shocked to see so many blind people at once—and I was certainly used to being around blind people.

As I Saw It

Figure 26: Article courtesy of *The Reporter*, Vacaville, CA

My mom and dad also attended a social club for the blind, which had a lot of overlap with members of the Blind Club. The social club wasn't as "official" as the Blind Club, but the social club had many more members who would attend on a regular basis. The social club was where new people who had just moved to the area could go to meet other blind people. Whenever my parents met a blind person they didn't know in the area, they would always invite them to come to both of the clubs. The social club was always scheduling activities, keeping all the members engaged, and looking forward to the next event.

My parents were even on a weekly bowling league. The bowling alley had handrails for use by the blind league bowlers. Each person would get their ball, then line up with the lane markings by holding the handrail. They would take a step and then release the ball, just like any other bowler. My parents weren't great bowlers. They went to have fun and socialize with their friends, so scores weren't so important. It was just for fun. The highest score on their team from one of the blind bowlers was 145. My dad's average score was 104.

Figure 27: My dad bowling
Photo courtesy of *The Reporter*, Vacaville, CA

My mom and dad took a camping trip to Camp Wawona every year with the Blind Club. The camp was inside Yosemite National Park, so they were able to stay in cabins and have their meals cooked for them. During the day, they would go on guided walking trips, horseback riding, or hiking through the wilderness. My mom was scared of horses, but my dad convinced her into taking a horseback ride. There was a lead horse who was assigned to a sighted person, and the horse at the back carried a sighted person, too. The horses were all trained to walk along, following each other along the trail. Most walking trail rides are uneventful.

It was a particularly hot day when my mom went on her ride, and the horses weren't all that happy about going. Midway through the ride, the horse my mom was riding started to get annoyed with the walk and just stopped—and my mom could not get her horse to continue. One of the guides was finally able to get my mom's horse going again, but the horse still didn't like it—and started wandering off the trail to head back to the stables. The horse was going under trees and around bushes that were brushing up against my mom's face, which scared her so badly she jumped off the horse. But she didn't jump deliberately off to the side of the horse, remembering how she got up, instead she panicked and jumped off the back of the horse and landed right on her behind. My poor mom was bruised from hip to hip and walked back to the start, because she wouldn't get back on that horse. When asked why she jumped off and didn't wait for the guides, she said, "I was scared the horse was taking me into the wilderness alone."

When my mom wasn't out doing social or advocacy activities with the blind clubs, she was happily taking care of the household. My mom did most everything. She got my brother and me ready for school in the mornings when we were younger, and when we got older she'd make sure we got out of bed on time when we turned off our alarms and fell back asleep. She cleaned the house and cooked the meals, still making sure to take time for her many friends. She was always talking to them on the phone, sometimes making plans to go out to lunch or out shopping with them. Often, her friends would come over to visit part of the day. She was very active, hardly ever alone, and rarely bored.

We'd all eat dinner together as a family and afterwards, mom would do the dishes while my brother and I did our homework. Then we'd turn on the TV and watch together as a family. The state had a whole library of Braille books and books on tape reserved for blind persons, so my parents read a lot when they weren't watching TV with us. My mom and dad filled out a questionnaire about what kinds of books they liked, and then the state would send a couple at a time in the mail. When books were sent back, more were delivered.

Our poor mailman was constantly carrying loads and loads of Braille and recorded books to our house. Sometimes, he'd put them in his bag and walk to do the neighborhood mail. But as time went on, he would simply leave the massive Braille books and the multiple-cassette cases in the mail car and deliver them at the end of the day, and do the same to pick up the ones my mom had sent back.

When my dad wasn't out doing activities with the blind clubs, he had his ham radio hobby. He was always talking on it or tinkering with it somehow. He'd meet people from all over the world via the airwaves. The 1970s was the era of the Cold War, and there was a lot of tension between Russia and the United States. My dad once found himself talking to a guy that he had just met for a few minutes, before asking where he was from. When the guy stated that he was from Russia and that he lived in Russia, my dad was stunned. For one, he was shocked that the signals were aligned so that he could communicate with someone so far away, and he also hadn't expected to find himself speaking with a Russian citizen because of the tensions between the two countries.

Suddenly, everyone listening to the same frequency wanted to talk to the guy from Russia. I could hear my dad talking excitedly, and when the signal faded away and they weren't able to communicate anymore, my dad came out and told us who he had been talking to. For months and months after that, my dad and all his ham radio friends tried to find the same guy to talk to him some more, but sadly, the signals didn't align for that to ever happen. My dad and his ham friends talked about it for years afterwards; it was a memorable night.

"DX"ING — Mr. Roy Phelps, blind amateur radio operator of station WB6FIS, Vacaville, tunes his set to talk "DX." Because he is sightless, the tuning knobs have been specially modified with knurled edges to help him find the proper frequencies. He has ham friends around the world who have no idea that Mr. Phelps cannot see. He recognizes operators by their voice, and calls many of his radio friends by name.

Figure 28: My dad on his ham radio ~1974
(Article courtesy of *Global Ranger*)

My dad's ham radio was a big part of his life; he was on it most of the time in the 70s and 80s, and went to the ham radio meetings and met most of his friends from using his ham radio. My dad had been talking on his radio for several months to a lieutenant in the Air Force stationed out at Travis Air Force Base near where we lived. My dad invited him to one of the ham radio club meetings one evening. When they met in person for the first time, the lieutenant was stunned to find out that my dad was blind.

After the meeting, they discussed writing a book together for other blind ham radio operators. The lieutenant got a lot of the information that was needed, and my dad Brailled the first edition of *DX and the Blind Ham*. It was a compilation of 80 pages of ham radio frequencies, bearings, and other data that blind hams needed so they could talk to other hams around the world. My dad, the lieutenant and another one of their ham friends donated their time to this project. My dad worked tirelessly for over a year Brailling all the data for the first copy.

BRAILLE — Fingers of the blind will soon be "reading" this book all over the world. It is the first time that blind operators have had this vital information available. The book is available to hams on a non-profit basis from Mr. Phelps of WB6FIS. Capt. Underhill, Lt. McVicar, and Mr. Phelps have donated their time and talents to make the book a reality.

Figure 29: My dad reading his book, *DX and the Blind Ham*
Article courtesy of *Global Ranger*

My dad was also a Military Auxiliary Radio System (MARS) operator in the 1970s and 1980s. The MARS program was a civilian group of licensed amateur (ham) radio operators who assisted the military with communications. The MARS program was used as an auxiliary emergency communication system during times of need. My dad explained to me that if there was ever a disaster or people ever needed to be evacuated, he would be able to use his ham radio to get any information needed for regular citizens and help out the local emergency services. Every year, the local MARS operators would coordinate and perform tests to make sure everyone knew what to do in case of an emergency and ensure that all the radios and equipment were working properly.

Before there were cell phones and internet chatting, my dad would also use his ham radio and our home phone so military personnel stationed overseas could communicate with their families back in the US. My dad connected the phone to his ham radio, and then he would be able to call the military personnel's families that were local, incurring no cost. It would take several ham radio operators to accomplish this task. Since we lived close to Travis Air Force Base, there were lots of calls that my dad was involved in personally. Most of the time, the military personnel were stationed overseas and the time differences would mean they would call their spouses or family members after midnight. My dad would stay up all night helping them call their families, because back then, servicemen and women rarely got to phone home.

It used to be that in order to be a ham radio operator and get a license, a person needed to be certified to read and send Morse code. At one time, my dad even taught Morse code to people applying for their ham radio licenses. He would spend hours and hours communicating over the air just using Morse code. I would walk into the room, and all I'd hear were beeps. I could only listen for a few minutes before I'd get so bored that I would walk away. I don't know how he sat for hours doing it, but then again, it was purposeful if he was teaching or responding, so I was just an observer and couldn't relate.

My dad gained a lot of weight from only having indoor activities for some time and not traveling so much on foot, so he joined Take Off Pounds Sensibly (TOPS). His TOPS meetings were held once a week, and he would weigh in and get and receive support for his goal. My dad started walking around the neighborhood then, to get a little exercise to help him lose weight. He'd walk around the block with his cane. The city was, ironically, implementing ADA modifications to all street corners to make them wheelchair accessible, and the modifications had started in our neighborhood. A few at a time, the workers removed the old sidewalk at the corner of the street that had a curb, and then put in a new piece of sidewalk that had a ramp for wheelchairs to get up.

One day my dad was out walking, and the workers had removed the corner of the sidewalk. There was only one construction barrier put in place and it had a flashing light. But my dad couldn't see the barrier or the flashing light, and worse, when he was swinging his cane, it had just missed contacting the barrier. My dad then fell into the hole that was left when they removed the portion of the sidewalk. He fell on his side and hit his shoulder on the edge of the sidewalk in that mishap. He was finally able to get up by himself using one hand, feel around for his cane, and make it back up to the house so he could get help.

He had to go to the emergency room because he was in so much pain, and there it was found that he had broken his shoulder and torn some cartilage. Surgery was required. He called the city several times, letting them know that he had fallen and was injured and that the holes were not barricaded adequately when the cement curbs were removed. He was persistent, just wanting to make sure that the city was on top of making sure other sites where they were replacing the sidewalk curbs were safe so that no one else would get hurt.

After all the calls that he made to the city, they asked him if he would like to be on the city's ADA Committee. That committee was responsible for making modifications throughout the city implementing the new ADA laws for disabled people. The city thought it would be a good idea to get the opinion of a disabled person about the plans the city had and what modifications the city was making for the ADA laws. The city wanted to make sure that the money they were spending was actually what the disabled people wanted or needed, and realized they didn't have that perspective on the team. So my dad aided the city in determining the importance and priority of some of the modifications they were planning to make.

Even though both my parents kept busy with advocacy, hobbies, and service, they always had time for my brother and me. When we were younger, my mom was always there to greet us when we came home from school. She would always ask us how our day went and was glad to see us when we walked in the door. She would have a snack ready for us because we were usually hungry when we got home. My mom and dad always kept my brother and me busy, too, when we were little. My dad Brailled a deck of cards, and they would play card games like Go Fish and Concentration with us. When we were older, my dad taught us how to play poker and blackjack, and sometimes we'd play for pennies.

Sunday nights were always family television nights. We'd take our baths after supper, and watch TV while we ate the evening snacks that my mom made for us. We'd have pudding, Jell-o, fruit cocktail, or popcorn to eat while we were watching TV, so we didn't go to bed hungry. They played board games with us, too. We used to play Sorry, Chutes and Ladders, and Trouble. My brother and I would have to read the cards or move the pieces around the board, but they would roll the dice themselves. We'd tell them what they rolled, and sometimes they could even move their own markers around the board. They would cheer and get just as excited as my brother and I did when we played. They made our lives fun. We never wanted to go to bed on family game nights.

My parents were more involved with us as kids than any of my friends' parents. My friends always wanted to come over to our house, actually, because my mom and dad always made them feel welcome and at home. My parents treated my friends just like they treated us. There was one movie theater in town, and every week they'd play a different movie. My mom would take us to the show, and let our friends come too.

My brother and I felt that we were the center of our parents' lives. They were never too busy to give us any attention we needed. They helped us when they could, and we helped them when we could. We were just a typical family, and there was nothing lacking in any of our lives. We were just a little different in the way we accomplished daily life.

Chapter 13
Where We Are Now

On Sunday, November 18, 2007, my mom and dad celebrated 47 wonderful years of life together. Unfortunately, the very next day, my dad passed away. His death was very sudden and unexpected, leaving us all in shock. Thank goodness, his death was quick and he did not suffer. He had been seen by his doctor the Friday before because he was having pain in his legs from his diabetes. His doctor gave him a referral to see a neurologist, but otherwise didn't see anything wrong with him. There were no signs of health trouble with my dad over that weekend. My mom and dad celebrated their anniversary quietly at home together, and everything was just as normal as it ever was.

My dad woke up Monday morning from a good night's rest. He got out of bed at his normal time and walked out of the bedroom. He didn't make it very far, though. He walked a few steps into the hallway and fell down. He yelled for my mom to help him get up, so my mom rushed to his side. She reached down and grabbed his hand, but each time she tried to pull him up she couldn't. My dad was so much bigger and heavier that she couldn't help him up—he pulled her down instead.

My mom said to my dad, "Roy, I need to get someone to help you get up." As soon as my mom told my dad she was going to get someone to help, my dad started frantically trying to get himself up off the floor, at least that's what my mom thought. She kept telling him, "Roy, stop that. You are going to hurt yourself. Let me get someone to help." But he continued to thrash around on the floor—and then there was silence. My mom thought that he had tried so hard to get up that he was resting for a moment. She called out, "Roy, are you okay?" When he didn't respond, she called 911.

She told the 911 operator that my dad had fallen and now he was silent on the floor. The 911 operator told my mom to go back and check to see if he was breathing, "Put your hand by his nose to see if you can feel any air coming out."

My mom came back to the phone, "I can't tell. He is making weird noises, gurgling sounds."

The operator said, "Check to see if he has a pulse. Do you know how to do that? Check on his neck below his ear next to his jaw."

My mom frantically said, "I don't know. I can't feel anything."

Then the 911 operator said, "An ambulance is already on its way."

Mom opened the door so that the EMTs could walk in, and then took a few steps to stand by my dad. Worried and not knowing what to do, my mom stood there in silence next to the man she had celebrated 47 long years with just the day before, hoping that the ambulance would arrive soon.

The EMTs rushed past her when they saw him lying on the floor, and started resuscitation efforts immediately. My mom could only listen helplessly to all the confusion that was going on next to her. She moved back a little bit to give them some room because that was the only thing she could do to contribute. She anxiously listened for any words she could understand to know what was happening. But the longer she listened, the more worried she became. After what seemed like hours had passed and the commotion stopped, she heard what she had dreaded. "Sorry, Mrs. Phelps, there is nothing more we can do. Your husband has passed." There was silence in the room and in her head, and she didn't hear anything that the EMTs were telling her after that. She fought hard to hold back the tears that were fighting to come out.

She didn't even notice that a police officer had walked into the house until he touched her arm and said, "I'm sorry for your loss. Is there a friend you can call to come over? He took her hand and walked her to the phone. She called the only number she could remember just then, that of her friend, Roseanne.

The police officer waited with my mom for Roseanne to arrive. The EMTs were packing up their equipment. My mom thought that the EMTs were going to take my dad's body with them, but they couldn't. The EMTs said, "We are not allowed to move a body unless the coroner has approved that it can be moved. There is a call out to the coroner, but he is out of town for the Thanksgiving holiday."

Roseanne arrived as fast as she could and at the same moment my mom's next door neighbor Carole came over to make sure everything was okay. When they walked into the house, they were both stunned to see my dad's body lying there on the floor, just as the paramedics had left it.

The coroner was finally reached, but he had to contact my dad's doctor to discuss my dad's health history, in order to determine that my dad's death was not suspicious. Talking to his doctor was the only way he could appraise the situation, since he was out of town. Both my mom and dad had been going to the same doctor for over 30 years, and again, dad had been to the doctor days earlier. When the doctor heard that my dad had passed, he drove immediately to fill out the death certificate so the coroner could give his approval for the mortuary to remove my dad's body. My dad's dead body lay in the hallway of our home for over five hours before the funeral director finally came.

My brother was in the army and deployed overseas when my dad died. I was living far away on the east coast by then. We came as quickly as we could. I arrived on Wednesday, and my brother arrived on Friday. My mom was never alone. She was constantly surrounded by friends until we could be by her side. Since my dad's death was ruled as due to natural causes, an autopsy was not mandatory by the coroner. My mom decided that she would be okay without knowing the exact cause of my dad's death and decided not to get an autopsy done privately.

My dad's service was held the week after Thanksgiving. There was no casket, open or closed, since his body had already been cremated. It was a memorial service, so I made signs with pictures in memory of my dad to put up at the service. There was also a table set up, full of memories of my parents, for attendees to see. Lots of people came to my dad's service: his ham radio friends, my mom and dad's friends from the Blind School, family friends, my mom's sisters and brother, and lots of cousins. The pastor of the church my mom had been attending officiated the service, which was held at the funeral home. It was a sad day, but nice to see all the people that we loved. My mom's family stayed for approximately a week.

My brother and I stayed for a couple of weeks, and afterward again, my mom wasn't alone after we left because her friends came over daily to keep her company.

Figure 30: Me, my mom, my brother at my dad's service.
We are standing behind the signs that I made.

After my dad's death, my mom was totally on her own—something she had not been her entire life. She was scared, especially since she had spent the last 47 years with my dad. Her friends were there with her most of the time, but she had lost many of them, too. She felt unsafe to be alone for a while and dealt with it the only way she knew how. There were delivery persons coming to her door from people sending flowers with their condolences for my dad's passing. The delivery person would knock on the door, but my mom wouldn't open the door at all. She'd ask who it was through the door. When they said they had a delivery, she told them "Just set it on the porch." She was afraid that someone was trying to lure her out of the house and persons unknown were waiting for her come out. So she wouldn't go out of her house to get the flowers until the next day, when she was sure no one was there.

She also kept my dad's greeting on the voicemail. Not because she still wanted to hear his voice, but because she didn't want anyone to know that she was living alone now. So every time I'd call or one of her friends would call and she wasn't home, we could never leave a message. I'd call to see how my mom was doing, but every time I heard my dad's voice, I'd start crying and would get so choked up that I couldn't speak to leave a message. So I'd just hang up. Her friends said they did the same thing. It took my mom a few months before she felt safe enough to be alone and recorded her own message.

It's been eight years since my dad's death. My mom still lives in the house where we grew up in Vacaville, California. She lives by herself, but is never alone. Her many friends come to visit almost on a daily basis. My mom and Josie are still great friends, talk to each other twice a day on the phone, and never miss a thing in each other's lives. They have a call in the morning to start their day, and always end the day with an evening call, too. My mom is still heavily involved with the blind clubs. She has a helper, Renee, who has been helping her for over 20 years. Renee makes out the bills every month and takes her shopping every week. Renee is more than just a helper; she has been there with my mom and for my parents always. She is now family.

My brother David went into the Army shortly after high school, and made his service to our country his lifetime career path. He retired at the end of 2015, at the rank of Sergeant First Class (SFC). He has had been deployed overseas to Germany, Iraq,

Afghanistan, Kosovo, and the first Gulf War. He was awarded two Bronze Stars for his service: Iraq in 2005 and Afghanistan in 2013. He met his wife, Irene, on one of his first deployments to Germany. They have been married for 26 years. She has been by his side and supported his career in the army throughout their marriage. They have five children: Rebecca (and spouse Charlie), Danielle (and spouse Anthony), David (and fiancée Alyse), Amanda (and spouse John), and Michael (and husband Timothy). They have nine grandchildren: Charlie, Catherine, Gabe, Isabelle, Noah, William, Cameron, and twins Charlotte and Olivia.

Unlike my brother, who made a career choice early, I got my dad's genes. I got out of high school and didn't know what to do. College wasn't even on my list of choices back then. I struggled with meaningless jobs, searching for meaning like my dad did. I finally figured out that I needed to go to school because I got fed up with working dead-end jobs. I worked in retail as a cashier, in a law firm as a transcriptionist, at a hospital as an assistant to the administrator, in a doctor's office transcribing, but nothing ever seemed enough. I tried court reporting school, but hated it and quit. After struggling for many years trying to figure it all out, I started taking classes at the local community college.

The first class I took was a class that offered testing to find out what my interests and abilities were, and what kinds of jobs would be the best fit for my personality. Clergy and accountant were the top fit from all the testing, but the results also showed that I could do pretty much anything that I wanted. That class wasn't very helpful. Everything I was interested in, all the sciences, needed lots of math. So I thought I'd start by taking math classes, to see how far I could get, because that would be what would hold me back. Every semester I took math, and every semester I got an A. Math came easy, actually. So I decided to get my degree in computer engineering, which is part computer science and part electrical engineering. I have been working as an engineer for over 17 years, and have loved every minute of it. I am always challenged and rarely bored. My hobby used to be hiking, but a knee injury stopped that. So my new hobby is writing.

I have a beautiful daughter, Jennifer, and son-in-law Victor, and two wonderful grandchildren, Brayden and Michael James, with another on the way. I live in California with four rescue cats: Nike, Bella, Sweetpea, and Red.

From the decision my two parents made, without sight, to forge ahead and create a life together, all of these paths were made possible.

Conclusion

LIFE DIDN'T ALWAYS GO AS PLANNED FOR either my mom or my dad. Their early lives were testaments to their strength and perseverance in spite of the challenges that life brought them. My dad, especially, had it pretty rough with all the tragedies that came up in his life. He had to learn what he had control over, so he knew what he could change—and what he really didn't have control over, so he could make peace with it and move on. My mom, in contrast, seemed more at peace knowing the difference earlier and took more of life in stride: going with the flow, accepting what came along. Some of that was just personality, and the rest was learning through experience.

I think that balance is what made their relationship work—their differences were somewhat complementary. Their backgrounds with blindness were different. My dad had seen a world without blindness, and he was able to share it with my mom. My mom was able to share her calmness and ease of life while being blind with him. They enhanced each other's lives, and together they knew they could overcome any obstacles that came their way.

That is part of why starting a family seemed like the right choice for them. They knew they would have more challenges than just the ordinary ones that came along with raising kids. They would also have their blindness to deal with every day, too. The support they gave each other from the beginning made the decision to start a family so much easier to make. The training at OCB gave them the confidence that they could handle any difficulties that came up in their lives, including the expected ones with raising children.

Raising kids was no easy feat, especially with me, but they did it well. They wanted everything for us and didn't want us to go without, like they had growing up in imperfect families during the Great Depression. They also didn't want their blindness to limit us or our family, so they took great strides to make sure that my brother and I had the best lives they could provide. We didn't go without. In fact, we usually had more than our friends did. We definitely had our parents' attention more than our friends had from theirs, because our parents made us the true center of their lives when we were younger. As my brother and I got older, we got involved more with our friends and started doing our own things just like most teenagers. And that's when my parents became a lot more active outside of our family, too. They led fulfilled and happy lives keeping busy with all their activities, helping the community, and raising us. They created the family neither of them was able to have when they were growing up.

Beyond being very capable and independent people and parents, they were remarkable role models for my brother and me. It wasn't so much the things they said to us, but how they lived their own lives that taught us how to live. They showed us that we could do most anything if we really wanted to. They showed us that if we really put our minds to it, anything was achievable, even the things that looked hard or had some barriers involved. They showed us also that life doesn't always go as planned, but that life goes on, and good things are possible after disappointment. They showed us that it isn't actually what happens to you in life, but how you handle it that makes your life what it becomes. They showed us by example that the choice is always ours to make.

Acknowledgements

I AM GRATEFUL FOR MY MOM AND DAD for all their love and the wonderful childhood they gave to me and my brother. You both have left me with a lot of wonderful memories to cherish.

I am grateful for my brother David who put up with my antics for so many years.

I am grateful for all my relatives who encouraged me to write this book and helped me remember the stories that I wrote about. I am thankful to all of you: Shirley, Linda, Larry, Nancy, Rick, Randy, Pauline, and Phil.

I am grateful for Josie telling stories about my mom and dad and her at the blind school. Thank you for being one of the greatest friends to our family and to my mom today.

I am grateful to all my friends who made my life eventful enough to write about.

I am grateful to my Aunt Pauline for all the wonderful photographs and articles that she saved for our memories knowing that my parents couldn't. RIP, Dear Pauline.

I am grateful for my editor Kate who helped take this good book to awesome. Thanks, Kate!

I am grateful to have such a wonderful friend, Niema, across the pond, who supported me and encouraged me throughout the writing process. Thanks, Niema!

I am grateful for Elliott because he helped me write this book without even knowing it.

About the Author

Laura Schriner was born in California. She has lived in California most of her life, except for 10 years spent in the Chicago suburbs and 5 years in the Washington DC suburbs. She has always been told by family and friends that she should write a book about her blind parents, so she finally listened to all the advice and wrote her first book: *As I Saw It*.

She is an avid hiker currently on hiatus working on her new writing hobby until she can recover from her knee injury. She has hiked all over the United States. Her most memorable hike was the one-day 24-mile rim-to-rim hike in Grand Canyon National Park.

She has a degree in computer engineering and has worked as an engineer for almost 20 years. She has a daughter, Jennifer, who is a nurse and lives in the Midwest. Laura currently lives in Southern California with her rescue cats.

For more information visit: www.lauraschriner.com

www.ingramcontent.com/pod-product-compliance
Lightning Source LLC
Chambersburg PA
CBHW032037290426
44110CB00012B/843